SAA

MANAGING
DISTRIBUTED DATA

IBM Series

K. BOSLER • *CLIST Programming* 0-07-006551-9

H. MURPHY • *Assembler for COBOL Programmers: MVS, VM* 0-07-044129-4

H. BOOKMAN • *COBOL II* 0-07-006533-0

P. MCGREW, W. MCDANIEL • *In-House Publishing in a Mainframe Environment, Second Edition* 0-07-046271-2

J. RANADE • *DB2: Concepts, Programming, and Design* 0-07-051265-5

J. SANCHEZ • *IBM Microcomputers Handbook* 0-07-054594-4

M. ARONSON • *SAS: A Programmer's Guide* 0-07-002467-7

J. AZEVEDO • *ISPF: The Strategic Dialog Manager* 0-07-002673-4

K. BRATHWAITE • *System Design in a Database Environment* 0-07-007250-7

M. CARATHANASSIS • *Expert MVS/XA JCL: A Complete Guide to Advanced Techniques* 0-07-009816-6

M. D'ALLEYRAND • *Image Storage and Retrieval Systems* 0-07-015231-4

R. DAYTON • *Integrating Digital Services* 0-07-016188-7

P. DONOFRIO • *CICS: Debugging, Dump Reading, and Problem Determination* 0-07-017606-X

T. EDDOLLS • *VM Performance Management* 0-07-018966-8

P. KAVANAGH • *VS COBOL II for COBOL Programmers* 0-07-033571-0

T. MARTYN • *DB2/SQL: A Professional Programmer's Guide* 0-07-040666-9

S. PIGGOTT • *CICS: A Practical Guide to System Fine Tuning* 0-07-050054-1

N. PRASAD • *IBM Mainframes: Architecture and Design* 0-07-050686-8

J. RANADE • *Introduction to SNA Networking: A Guide to VTAM/NCP* 0-07-051144-6

J. RANADE • *Advanced SNA Networking: A Professional's Guide for Using VTAM/NCP* 0-07-051143-8

J. TOWNER • *CASE* 0-07-065086-1

S. SAMSON • *MVS: Performance Management* 0-07-054528-6

B. JOHNSON • *MVS: Concepts and Facilities* 0-07-032673-8

P. MCGREW • *On-Line Text Management: Hypertext* 0-07-046263-1

L. TOWNER • *IDMS/R* 0-07-065087-X

A. WIPFLER • *Distributed Processing in the CICS Environment* 0-07-071136-4

A. WIPFLER • *CICS Application Development Programming* 0-07-071139-9

J. RANADE • *VSAM: Concepts, Programming, and Design, Second Edition* 0-07-051244-2

J. RANADE • *VSAM: Performance, Design, and Fine Tuning, Second Edition* 0-07-051245-0

SAA

MANAGING DISTRIBUTED DATA

Michael Killen

McGraw-Hill, Inc.

New York St. Louis San Francisco Auckland Bogotá
Caracas Hamburg Lisbon London Madrid
Mexico Milan Montreal New Delhi Paris
San Juan São Paulo Singapore
Sydney Tokyo Toronto

Library of Congress Cataloging-in-Publication Data

Killen, Michael.
    SAA, managing distributed data / Michael Killen.
       p.   cm. -- (IBM series)
    Includes index.
    ISBN 0-07-034608-9
    1. IBM Systems Application Architecture. 2. Distributed data
bases. 3. Data base management. I. Title. II. Series.
QA76.9.A73K55   1991
004' .36--dc20   91-26996
                                                        CIP

1 2 3 4 5 6 7 8 9 0 DOC/DOC 9 7 6 5 4 3 2 1

ISBN   0-07-034608-9

*The sponsoring editor for this book was Jeanne Glasser, the editing
supervisor was Jim Halston, and the production supervisor was
Pamela A. Pelton*

Printed and bound by R. R. Donnelley & Sons.

*Subscription information to BYTE Magazine: Call
1-800-257-9402 or write Circulation Dept., One
Phoenix Mill Lane, Peterborough NH 03458.*

Contents

Preface

We are in the Decade of Innovation. A key requirement of corporations during this period will be to empower knowledge workers to identify and seize rapidly developing business opportunities. The key requirement for information systems management will be to build the information systems that will empower the corporation's technical and marketing experts, product planners, program managers, change managers, and executives. The companies who excel at this will have the best chance to prosper in this decade.

In the Decade of Innovation, opportunities will pop up and dash by like clay targets with the speed of nano-technology, allowing us little time to act. Companies such as Digital Equipment, IBM, Hewlett-Packard, and Sun Microsystems already must bring a new workstation to market in less than a year, once they determine the market requirements, or they miss the opportunity. The ideas for AT&T's entry into the credit card market and Motorola's plans to develop a worldwide satellite-based personal communications network developed but a few short years ago. Companies are going to have to recognize opportunities and move very fast during this period.

The Decade of Innovation has largely been created by the wide-scale use of information systems technology, and advances in information systems technology will be required to exploit the opportunities of the age.

The three decades that preceded this one each had a management theme—"planning" in the 1960s, "productivity" in the 1970s, and "quality" in the 1980s. In the 1990s, MIS must adopt a different focus.

During the decade of "planning," management focused on developing the corporation's ability to plan its future. They applied computer systems technology to obtain the information needed to plan, to control, and to manage. They automated "back office" functions—accounting and financial departments—to collect data on the corporation's operations.

In the 1970s, businesses concentrated on "productivity." North American and Western European companies had to focus on productivity to meet the challenges of lower labor rates from the Pacific Rim and emerging Western European suppliers. Companies embraced the concepts of just-in-time manufacturing (JIT), flexible manufacturing, and outsourcing. They also applied computer-aided manufacturing (CAM) to assist purchasing, production control, and accounting departments to plan and control the manufacturing process.

In the 1980s, managers focused on improving "quality." Some developed Western companies implemented Deming's[1] quality circles and Juran's[2] quality control. Companies invested billions of dollars in tools to improve the quality of products, and they invested more to build products faster—computer-aided design (CAD), computer-aided engineering (CAE), computer-aided publishing (CAP), computer-aided software engineering (CASE). The stampede of U.S. corporations to win the Malcolm Baldrige Award at the beginning of the 1990s was a result of the "quality" mindset of the 1980s.

In the Decade of Innovation, MIS must, for starters, continue to accomplish all of the above, but they must also add a new focus. They must concentrate on building systems that enable the corporation's knowledge workers to identify opportunities, select a winner, and exploit it before the competition can. They must build systems that provide knowledge workers with a new window to the world of opportunities. That system must provide a new view of the marketplace and the corporation's capabilities.

Historically, MIS has built information systems that give knowledge workers information about the marketplace. Many of these systems focused on sales activity or forecasting. Few systems contained details about the customer's goals, objectives, people, and competitors. What are needed now are systems that provide a step function improvement in the quality, relevance, and usability of information about market opportuni-

---

1. W. E. Deming, who first introduced quality control in Japan in 1950.
2. In 1954 in Japan, J. M. Duran introduced the concept of quality control as a managerial tool to improve performance.

ties. What are needed are systems that provide knowledge workers the information they need to identify the best opportunities faster.

MIS must also focus on building systems that enable knowledge workers to focus inward on a company's capabilities. Companies capture little information, historically, about their capabilities. They have information about the company's resources and physical assets—things, employees, revenue—and some information about the status of projects. But MIS has not built the systems that provide information about a company's processes—the way they do things, the way they create. Processes are directly related to capabilities. Improve a company's processes and you improve performance.

If knowledge workers are to improve processes, they need good information. MIS professionals must now create the systems that provide knowledge workers with not just more information but information that has quality, is relevant, and is usable—information that will improve a company's processes. Such systems, I believe, will be based on systems that manage distributed data bases.

IBM will play a role in many companies' plans during the Decade of Innovation. IBM's framework for the commercial information systems environment in the 1990s is Systems Application Architecture (SAA). Distributed data base systems are an extremely important part of SAA.

A distributed data base system, by my definition, is one that (1) allows for access and update of data across multiple computer systems platforms, (2) enables users to access and update data on multiple systems with a single transaction, without knowing where the data exist or the type of system on which they exist, and (3) provides the security and performance needed for this level of computing.

This book will review SAA and IBM's distributed data base strategy. I hope it will be helpful to the information systems professionals who are responsible for building the generation of systems that will empower knowledge workers in the Decade of Innovation.

Acknowledgments

Two people worked very hard to help create this book.

I thank S. S. (Tim) Tyler, partner of the System Consulting Consortium, Inc., who worked with me on an earlier project and introduced me to many of the concepts of distributed data bases. In my opinion, Tim is one of the best thinkers in the computer industry today.

And I thank the editor and director of Technical Publications for Killen & Associates, Inc., Edie Gaertner, for her hard work in pulling this manuscript together.

Trademarks

Apple, HyperCard, and Macintosh are registered trademarks of Apple Computer, Inc.

UNIX is a registered trademark of AT&T Co.

CompuServe and Online Today are registered trademarks of CompuServe Incorporated.

DEC, VAX, and VAX/VMS are registered trademarks and DECnet is a trademark of Digital Equipment Corporation.

Kodak is a registered trademark of Eastman Kodak Company.

GE is a registered trademark of General Electric.

Application System/400, AIX, IBM, PS/2, and OS/2 are registered trademarks of International Business Machines Corporation. AD/Cycle, AS/400, DB2, ES/9370, ImagePlus, Micro Channel, MVS/XA, OS/400, QMF, RISC System/6000, SQL, SAA, System/360, System/370, and Systems Application Architecture are trademarks of International Business Machines Corporation.

Lotus 1-2-3 is a registered trademark of Lotus Development Corporation.

Microsoft and MS-DOS are registered trademarks and Windows is a trademark of Microsoft Corp.

ORACLE is a trademark of Oracle Corp.

ROLM is a trademark of ROLM Company.

Sun Microsystems is a registered trademark of Sun Microsystems, Inc.

WordStar is a registered trademark of WordStar International Corp.

SAA

MANAGING
DISTRIBUTED DATA

1
Introduction

Since Systems Application Architecture (SAA) was announced nearly four years ago, I have considered this to be the single most important announcement ever made in the computer industry, and I have treated it as such. Since the announcement, I have analyzed all other computer industry developments as entities that must coexist in what will be the SAA environment of the 1990s. Moreover, I have concluded that these entities (such as UNIX-based systems) will find an increasingly hostile environment, in which survival will eventually depend on establishing a symbiotic relationship with SAA.

In fact, I believe that the credibility gap between the computer industry and its customer base is increasing. The promised benefits of computer technology have not materialized. Costs cannot be justified by tangible savings. Increased volume and velocity of information are no substitute for quality. Data, in and of themselves, have no intrinsic value. All too frequently, complex systems development projects fail, and simple "solutions" simply don't work. There is increasing awareness that computer systems can represent vulnerability and loss of control. This vulnerability will become sharply focused in the 1990s as traditional paper-based systems are replaced and knowledge-based systems emerge.

The real solution to the above problems, and the key to IBM's SAA strategy, is distributed data base management. Information systems are only as good as the quality of the supporting data. The microprocessor revolution has ensured that data will be distributed, whether or not they can be managed in terms of synchronization, integrity, and security. These

1

are technical problems that are either misunderstood or ignored by vendors. At the very heart of SAA lies IBM's solution to distributed data base management. If IBM's solution works, the 1990s will be the dawning of the "information age." If it doesn't, the computer "slump" of the 1980s will look like the "good old days."

In a very real sense, IBM has bet the company on SAA. Unfortunately, whether you are a customer or a competitor, IBM has also bet your company. We all have a vested interest in seeing IBM's SAA succeed. When SAA was announced, I was optimistic that IBM had an appropriate strategy and a good chance of succeeding. Today, SAA remains an enigma to both IBM's customers and its competitors. In addition, IBM's tactics and product announcements in the last two years have caused additional concerns. The positioning of the AS/400, OfficeVision, ImagePlus, AD/Cycle, the Repository, Cooperative Processing, and AIX have failed to inspire confidence that IBM is really focused on the fundamental problem—distributed data base management—or is prepared to solve the problem quickly and efficiently.

To understand these developments and my concerns, we need to return to basics and understand the problems.

Today, almost 40 percent of U.S. capital is spent on computer technology, and many corporate executives are becoming dissatisfied with the return on their investments. The expectations of investors in computer technology have been raised by vague concepts such as the "information age," which effectively ignore practical economic reality, and by information systems "solutions," which have been partial at best and in many cases simply do not address real problems. In fact, indications are that many information systems "solutions" are themselves part of the problem. While this has been demonstrated by well-documented cases of spectacular systems failures, a more insidious outcome is that one can invest an enormous amount of capital and human effort in computer technology and actually obtain information of inferior quality. These unfortunate facts go well beyond the quarterly results of computer companies in their implications for the economy of the United States.

Three major issues must be addressed to understand the problem:

(1) The proper distribution of processing power and data over a hierarchical network consisting of mainframes, minicomputers, and intelligent workstations

(2) The productivity of office workers at the individual, work unit, and institutional levels

(3) The effective integration of data, information, and knowledge within the organization

The most important technical issue being addressed by SAA is distributed data base (DDB) management. This book analyzes IBM's distributed data base strategy as an integral part of its greater SNA (Systems Network Architecture)/SAA strategy and within the larger framework of the major issues identified above. This is an extremely complex undertaking in its own right, and the conclusions and recommendations alone take up nearly 30 pages. It is extremely important to read about DDB and the IBM SAA strategy together. In my opinion, they are the most important issues confronting the information systems industry. It is extremely difficult to summarize SAA and DDB briefly, except to state that:

- SAA is necessary to provide a common view of IBM's diverse hardware-software offerings. Placed in the context of the major issues, it addresses those depicted in Figure 1.1.

- Distributed data base management is necessary to provide this common view and to maintain the quality of data in a distributed processing environment.

- Distributed data base management is complex, and complex technical problems have not been solved.

- IBM has a distributed data base management plan that recognizes the complexity of these problems and provides the potential for an "industrial-strength" solution.

- IBM's distributed data base management solution will integrate operating systems and data base management systems (DBMSs) so tightly that IBM's SNA/SAA network will function as a single system that views "connected," non-IBM systems as "peripherals."

- If IBM is successful in its distributed data base management strategy, I conclude that:

    - It will be successful in establishing IBM account control among a broad segment of the user community because it solves real problems of data quality that are essentially being ignored by competitors.

    - It will have substantial market impact on competitive hardware and software products.

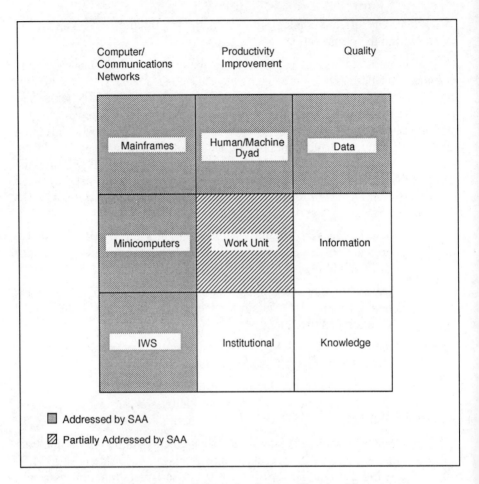

Figure 1.1 – An Information Systems Planning Map

Source: Killen & Associates, Inc.

I conclude that IBM: (1) has a carefully conceived technical solution to the distributed data management problem, (2) has committed the necessary resources to implement the SAA distributed data base strategy, and (3) will be generally successful in that strategy.

Therefore, it is recommended that both competitors and users:

- Adopt an acceptable paradigm that includes the major issues defined above.

- Take both SAA and DDB seriously.
- Understand data, information, and knowledge and the importance of their effective integration.
- Develop a strategic plan in response to IBM's SNA/SAA/DDB strategy.
- Organize to execute and monitor that plan.
- Set up a contingency plan to be executed in the event that the assumptions concerning IBM's SNA/SAA/DDB strategy must be adjusted.

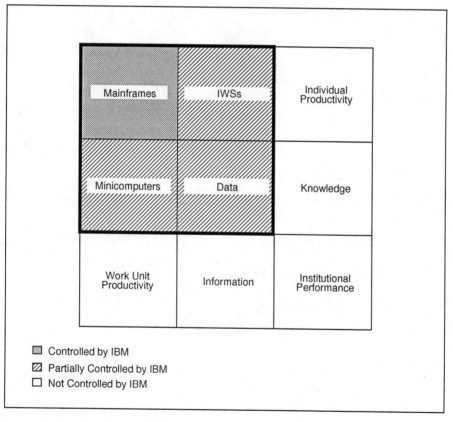

Figure 1.2 – Strategic Reversal of IBM's SNA/SAA/DDB Strategy

Source: Killen & Associates, Inc.

If the above recommendations are executed with care, I anticipate that the major issues can be rearranged to draw on IBM's solution to the distributed data base problem so that IBM's network can be effectively viewed as the distributed data base "peripheral" for the information and knowledge networks of the 1990s. This could achieve strategic reversal and put IBM in something of a box (Figure 1.2).

2

SAA Review

The concept of a distributed data base is the very essence of SAA, and neither the concept nor the need for a DDB is very well understood by vendors or users. This book will provide some understanding of these issues. To accomplish this, I will first briefly review some concepts of SAA.

2.1   THE FOUR ESSENTIAL ELEMENTS

SAA consists of four related elements: (1) Common User Access, (2) Common Programming Interface, (3) Common Communications Support, and (4) Common Applications (which will be developed adhering to the standards established in the first three). The general diagram of the architecture, presented in Figure 2.1, essentially displays IBM's top-level view for developers of the applications systems that are to be distributed across computer/communications networks.

(1) Common User Access (CUA) will be designed for the end user and optimized for the particular workstation.

(2) The Common Programming Interface (CPA) will consist of a variety of languages and services.

  – Languages will include "common" higher-level languages, an applications generator, a procedures language, and a 5GL (fifth-generation language).

7

– Services will consist of a data base interface, a query interface, a presentation and dialog interface, and distributed services.

(3) Common Communications Support will consist of extensions to existing communications architectures, will be based upon SNA and "selected" international standards, will support distributed functions, and will be consistent with open communications architecture.

(4) These enabling elements of SAA may be viewed as a shell with which the users and developers (programmers) of common applications interact. The shell serves as a shield from the complexity that currently exists among IBM's diverse hardware and software product offerings.

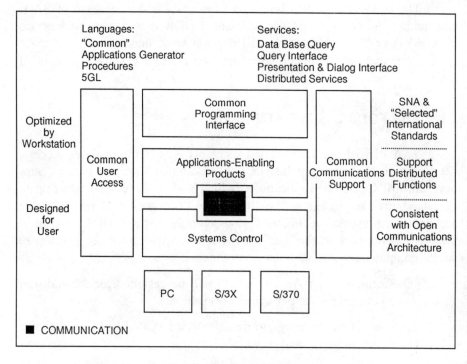

Figure 2.1 – SAA Diagram

Source: IBM

It is important to remember that substantial complexity exists under the shell in the form of:

- The operating systems to support the "major IBM computing environments" (previously designated as the System/370, the System/3X, and personal computers).

- The applications-enabling products, which include compilers, interpreters, and translators for languages; various data base management systems (and presumably any hardware products to support them); and a mixed bag of applications development tools and aids.

- The central "black box" of data base and communications products necessary to control the data information flow both within and among the major computing environments and with all the elements of SAA.

This top-level overview of SAA shows clearly that it is an exceptionally complex systems integration effort at many levels. Conceptually, IBM is attempting to portray both the meaning of and need for SAA to its customers with some new terminology—cooperative processing and information reservoirs.

2.2   ASSOCIATED IBM CONCEPTS

Since the early days of computers, IBM has attempted to distinguish its products from those of competitors through terminology. For example, the IBM 705 console proudly displayed that it was an "Electronic Data Processing Machine," and its character (byte) representation and organization were familiar to anyone who had ever seen a punch card. This set data processing apart from the "scientific computing" done on "binary" machines, through which Univac had become a generic name for computers.

Fred Brooks, one of the primary architects of the IBM System/360, once stated (concerning systems software) that "we seem to have more terms than concepts here." There is certainly an element of that in trying to establish the differences between "distributed processing" and the new terms "cooperative processing" and "information reservoirs." However, from IBM's point of view, there are some crucial distinctions. This becomes apparent when we see what IBM means by "cooperative processing," illustrated in Figure 2.2.

The term "distributed processing" started with minicomputers and has been traditionally associated with off-loading from IBM mainframes. It would be fair to state that IBM has been fighting a war against distributed processing for more than 15 years. The fact that IBM has drawn up the wagons around mainframes is clearly illustrated in Figure 2.2. The large central mainframe is depicted as an "extension of resources" for an intelligent workstation (IWS), providing virtual disk and virtual print. No mention is made of off-loading applications to the desktop, much less the fact that many mainframe applications were developed when the mainframe had less processing power than is now available on the desktop.

Then the IWS is depicted as having access to distributed data on a S/3X that provides virtual file (as distinguished from virtual disk), query and extract (hopefully between mainframe and S/3X as well as between IWS and departmental processor), and distributed data bases (an important enough subject to prompt this book). Once again, it is important to recognize that cooperative processing at that level does not explicitly mention the off-loading of applications from mainframes, nor is it necessarily implicit in certain forms of data distribution.

Only when the IWS is attached to the ES/9370 minicomputer is off-loading specifically mentioned, and then it is only between the two. The listed functions (distributed application services, complex programs, information editing and document distribution, and store and forward distribution) do not give any indication that IBM expected the ES/9370 to off-load any significant processing from the host mainframe.

Therefore, IBM's cooperative processing is indeed somewhat different from distributed processing as it has been advocated by minicomputer vendors for many years. IBM has been largely successful in combating distributed processing over the years because of one very specific problem— distributed data bases. The problem of the DDB has, to this point, defied adequate technical solution. And even if minicomputer vendors understand the problem, they largely ignore it.

The fact that, as an industry, we can bandy a term like "distributed processing" around for so long without recognizing the importance of the data that are to be distributed is frightening. IBM, in some of its customer presentations, has given an even broader perspective to the problem by referring to computer/communications networks as "information reservoirs." This term includes not only the structured data in data bases, but also the information (reports, memoranda, graphics, etc.) that can be generated, stored, and distributed over the network. The effective management

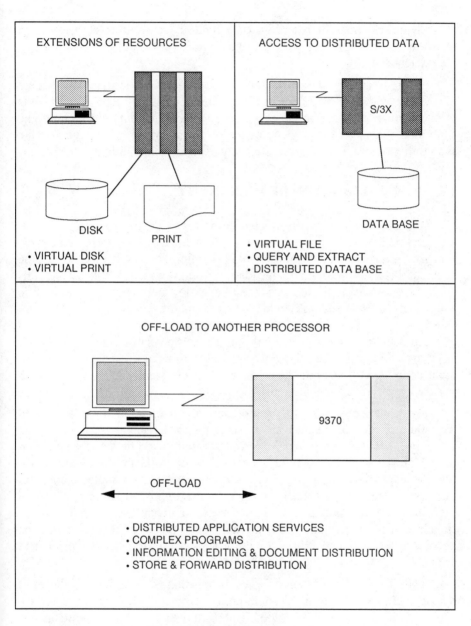

Figure 2.2 – Cooperative Processing

Source: IBM

of such an information reservoir is beyond the current state of systems
software technology, but at least the requirements are not being completely ignored.

More recently, the term "enterprise processing system" has come
into vogue within IBM. Fundamentally, this is a macro view of the results
of the proper distribution of processing power and data throughout the
enterprise. Thus, terminology marches on ahead of both concept and the
availability of systems software tools to permit implementation.

2.3   SYSTEMS SOFTWARE HIERARCHY

In the beginning, man created computer with no thought that "telling the thing what to do" would be a problem. Computer lore relates the
surprise that accompanied the first programming "bugs." It rapidly became
apparent that "programming" the darned things was a problem, and this
chore was usually relegated to somewhat junior members of the scientific
community. Bill Woodbury (while at the Institute for Advanced Study at
Princeton) recalls telling John von Neumann (mathematician and creator
of the precursor to today's general-purpose computer) that he would never
program a computer. He felt (and may feel to this day) that you didn't program computers, you built them to do what you wanted them to do (such
as solving differential equations).

However, man was so enamored with his creation that he decided
the solution was to create systems software to accompany the hardware.
The thought was that this would permit computers to "be fruitful and mul-
tiply." Then the problems really started. Not only did the hardware multi-
ply, the bugs did also. Since being thrown out of the computer Garden of
Eden, software has supposedly never caught up with hardware in terms of
exploiting the full potential of this wonderful invention. However, occasionally, the two-headed software-hardware monster seems intent on
devouring the best capabilities of those responsible for "telling it what to
do."

The foregoing is intended to point out that SAA is merely the most
recent attempt to "solve the programming problem" and set the stage for
viewing software somewhat globally. Fundamentally, the software hierarchy (Figure 2.3) is defined as being anything that is not hardware—and
that includes the human beings who are connected to computer/communi-
cations networks.

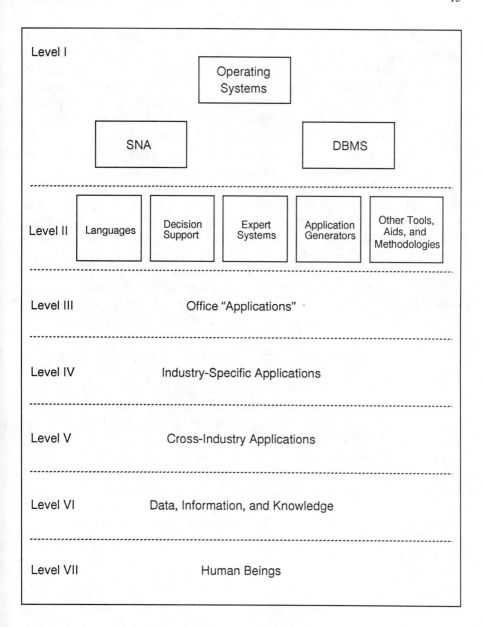

Figure 2.3 – The Software Hierarchy

Source: Killen & Associates, Inc.

Level I of the software hierarchy includes the systems services that are fundamental to the computer/communications network. In a distributed data base environment, operating systems, communications, and DBMSs must be tightly integrated. Indeed, the generic term "operating system" was once sufficiently broad to cover all of Level I. IBM may have competitive reasons for wanting to exercise tight control over Level I software, but there are also sound technical reasons for its doing so.

Level II represents the application-enabling functions that draw on the systems services. In terms of general system theory, as described by Ludwig von Bertalanffy in *General System Theory* (George Braziller, 1968), this is a level of differentiation. Highly specialized languages will be necessary even if we are able to translate "natural" language—witness specialized dictionaries for the professions. Decision support systems depend on the types of decisions being made—strategic, tactical, real-time, etc. Expert systems by definition address quite narrow domains. And, unless applications generators recognize the requirements of other Level II components in terms of response time and general quality, they will continue to wallow in the backwaters of the systems development process.

Level III office "applications" have become the victim of personal computer hype and misunderstanding. Word processing, electronic mail, and "desktop publishing" may be true office applications, but spreadsheets obviously belong in Level II, and DBMSs belong in Level I. In a distributed data base environment, this will become apparent quite rapidly. The most promising current application in the office is the control, reduction, and (in some cases) elimination of paper documents. Since "office automation" seems directed toward producing ever-increasing quantities of "pretty" documents (and selling printers), this is not an especially popular point of view. This subject will be addressed in more detail later, but it should be pointed out that paper "information bases" are currently being distributed in an uncontrolled manner. That is the essence of the office productivity problem.

Level IV includes industry-specific applications (sometimes called turnkey systems). IBM has stated that the first SAA common applications will address the office and that these will be followed by industry-specific applications. This level of application recognizes that some office processes are industry-dependent and reasonably well defined; for example, the clearing of checks or the processing of insurance claims. It is significant that when an office process is clearly understood, the reduction (or elimination) of paper documents normally becomes a primary systems objective. IBM has frequently used insurance systems as an example when presenting cooperative processing and distributed data bases.

Level V is the "package programs" that are relatively industry-dependent. Most of these applications have been associated with accounting functions that have traditionally had a solid systems foundation in terms of data collection and entry, transaction processing, and even reporting. End-user computing, applications "prototyping" with new development tools, and the inevitable distribution of data are beginning to cause serious concern among both internal and external auditors. This concern is well founded.

Level VI is a significant departure from the more conventional software described in Levels I through V. Computer programs must have structure (in the broadest sense of the word) if they are to operate at all. The data on which programs operate, the information produced by computer processing, and the human knowledge applied around these artificial systems are all much "softer." The old saw about "garbage in, garbage out" remains as true as ever. Advances in hardware technology and usability, as represented in the first five levels of the software hierarchy, do not necessarily contribute to improved quality of data, information, and/or knowledge. It is a lesson that seems to need constant reinforcement. Data, information, and knowledge will be discussed in more detail later in this book.

Finally, at Level VII we have human beings, who are, and shall continue to be, the most important components of any information system. This should not be construed as the gratuitous remark of a humanist—it also serves to fix responsibility. Human beings remain the least predictable (that is to say, reliable) components of the information system, and any well-designed information system will not only recognize this fact but also take advantage of the flexibility of this human software. Indeed, if there is one message this book will attempt to get across, it is that the human information network should be designed first.

Presently, the various levels of the software hierarchy are all closely associated with specific hardware systems. At Level I, there are mainframe, minicomputer, and microprocessor operating systems; and at Level VII, the human beings can usually identify "their" computer as falling into one of these categories. Software at the in-between levels is also associated with and closely tied to specific levels of the processor hierarchy.

Simply stated, the purpose of SAA is to make the hardware hierarchy transparent to the software hierarchy.

2.4   DISTRIBUTED PROCESSING

Sometime in the 1960s, a person responsible for the systems software support of a large IBM OS/360 installation met a former colleague from the IBM Research Center and asked him what he was working on. The colleague stated that he was working on scheduling algorithms for time-sharing systems. The systems support manager stated that it had been his experience that for batch jobs the best scheduling algorithm was to get the short jobs out of the system as soon as possible (in other words, give them priority), and that he didn't see any reason this would not apply in a time-sharing system.

About six months later, the systems support manager again met the colleague, who stated: "Oh, by the way, I have solved the scheduling algorithm problem. It is best to get the short jobs out of the system as fast as possible." When reminded about the conversation six months earlier, the colleague calmly stated: "But I can prove it!"

We now have a comparable situation with computer/communications networks. For the last 15 years, some have been advocating a three-tiered "proper" hierarchy of processors for distributed processing (Figure 2.4). This hierarchy has been based on cost and price–performance rather than on architecture, and it has stood the test of time remarkably well. The diagram has been published through numerous sources on many occasions, and it has been presented to many audiences, including IBM and various other computer vendors.

The hardware-software technology for industry-specific implementation of such distributed systems has been available since the early 1970s. Indeed, the structure of the "proper" hierarchical network was prompted by the fundamental requirements of servicing microprocessor-based point-of-sale terminals. IBM, in announcing SNA, ignored the minicomputer level in favor of 3790 controllers, which had limited capability for distributing functions from mainframes. The 8100 was not much better, and its failure as a true engine of distributed processing was predictable. (In a 1979 analysis of the 8100, one analyst stated: "The 8100 appears to be a super controller dressed up to be a minicomputer . . . the engine itself may be too weak to drive the system.")

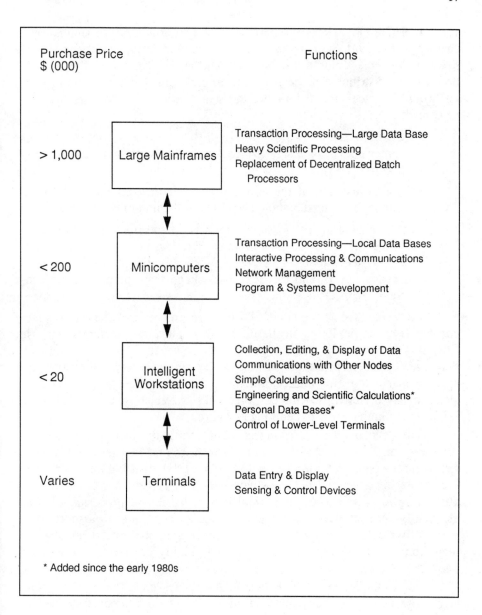

Figure 2.4 – The Processing Hierarchy

Source: Killen & Associates, Inc.

In 1978, Dr. Allan L. Scherr published an article on distributed processing in the *IBM Systems Journal* ("Distributed Data Processing," *IBM Systems Journal*, Volume 17, No. 4). The article addressed the general problems of distributed processing and properly concluded that the following would be necessary if the advantages of distributed processing were to be gained:

- Centralized design of the system data base and control over its content, level of usage (by particular elements of the application programs), synchronization, recovery, and distribution.

- The structuring of the application program itself into pieces that can be distributed and the definition of the unit of distribution.

- And once a distributed application is up and running, central control of the level of the programs, the data bases, and the operating systems themselves. (This would require at least a central library control and distribution package that operates in the central node of the system.)

Dr. Scherr then concluded: "Distributed processing offers an unprecedented level of flexibility in the design of applications systems. Because flexibility is inevitably a two-edged sword, however, it is more necessary than ever before to proceed with understanding and with deliberate, manageable plans. It is for this reason more than any other that the cornerstone of any effective distributed processing system must be the ability to implement a high degree of centralized control."

This is a sound conclusion that remains true to this day. All my presentations of the hierarchical network have been prefaced by the advice to first centralize and then proceed with the "orderly" distribution of processing to the lower levels in the network. IBM's problem has been that, in attempting to solve the general problems of distributed processing, it has essentially "protected" its customers by putting them on such a short hardware-software leash that precious little processing has ever been distributed from the large central mainframes. A highly centralized "star-type" network has been the result.

For example, in 1989, Killen & Associates undertook a consulting engagement for a company that had one of the world's largest networks of IBM 8100s operating under the Distributed Processing Programming Executive (DPPX) operating system. The company had spent 10 years making DPPX "work" and found itself with multiple 8100s installed at all its network nodes, with some of these multiple 8100s required for a single application (with resulting scheduling and coordination problems). The company was (of necessity) in the process of "converting" its DPPX applications from 8100s to 9370s (IBM having dropped the 8100 as the predictable failure it was). The frustration with making "IBM-style" distributed processing work was apparent, and the company was in the process of deciding whether to return to a centralized operation. IBM had prevailed at the expense of its loyal customer.

The personal computer revolution changed the networking situation, and two-tiered networks, either micro-mainframe or micro-minicomputer, have become quite common. This distribution of processing and data has not been "orderly," and the problems anticipated by Scherr have proven all too real. I think that in this chaotic environment, IBM's highly centralized strategy makes more sense than it ever has in the past.

In 1987, Dr. Scherr published another article on distributed processing in the *IBM Systems Journal* ("Structures for Networks of Systems," *IBM Systems Journal*, Volume 26, No. 1). In that article he pointed out that with the introduction of minicomputers, and especially with the advent of personal computers, there has been increasing debate about the proper role of mainframes, departmental processors, and the desktop personal computer. He further stated that there have been arguments that "one or more of these classes of machine and/or usage will disappear."

After a well-reasoned review of both the history and potential of distributed data processing, Dr. Scherr concludes: "In this paper, we have looked at a full spectrum of possibilities. It is difficult to escape the conclusion that each type of system has a significant role to play, and it is difficult to imagine technology changes that would eliminate any of the types. Each type of system represents unique advantages that argue strongly for its usage. Thus, we conclude that multiple-tier systems will be in general use, particularly in large corporations, for many years to come."

Once again, my problem analysis and practical experience have been confirmed by a level of research that surpasses my resources. I am impressed that this level of effort preceded IBM's announcement of SAA.

2.5   SUMMARY ANALYSIS

A number of major information systems issues exist today (Figure 2.5). SAA addresses the classic distributed processing problem, productivity at the human/machine dyad, and the data quality problem. It promises to begin to address the work unit productivity problem. It does not specifically address the problems of information and knowledge quality or how these contribute to institutional productivity. (The term "institutional" is used because it is broader than "enterprise.") This is not a criticism of SAA, which is already ambitious beyond the comprehension of practically all computer users, most vendors, many technical "experts," and probably some of those who are committed to making it happen.

SAA is the most complex systems software endeavor ever to be undertaken. The ultimate objective is the age-old quest to make the physi-

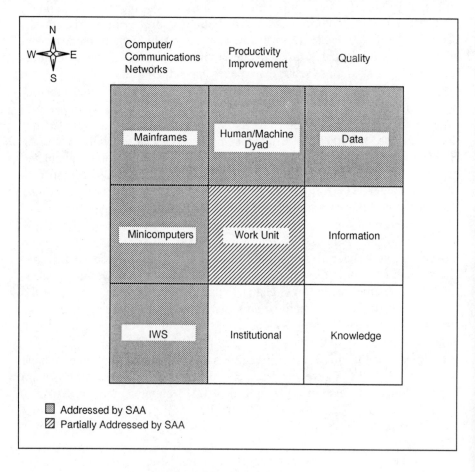

Figure 2.5 – SAA Directions

Source: Killen & Associates, Inc.

cal mechanism and geographic location of both data and processing transparent to end users. "'Tis a consummation devoutly to be wish'd . . . ," but it ain't going to be easy.

The fundamental problem is the high entropy inherent in distributed data bases. This problem centers in the NE box of the Information Systems Planning Map (Figure 2.5). While information and knowledge quality are not addressed by SAA, the emphasis upon data quality is appropriate since data quality is the essential foundation for addressing the other two issues.

Dr. Scherr recognized this problem in his 1978 paper cited above; thus, we must assume that IBM is serious about having an "architected" solution to the problems of distributed data bases. This book will describe the distributed data base problem, analyze what appears to be IBM's solution, assess IBM's chances of success, and evaluate what this means to users and vendors.

3

Data Base Management Systems

Data base management systems have replaced programming languages as the most emotionally charged topic of discussion among computer scientists, pseudo-scientists, "experts," and all the assorted theorists who like to air their opinions, prejudices, and vituperation in public. I do not intend to become tangled in this muddle, but I will at least explain the reason why I prefer to spell data base as "data base" rather than "database." (The fact that even the spelling cannot be agreed upon is indicative of why I prefer to stay above most of the controversy.) The reason I prefer "data base" is simple: data bases must be distinguished from information bases and knowledge bases, and I prefer not to start using "informationbase" and "knowledgebase" for purposes of consistency. With that clarification, we can proceed with the business at hand.

3.1   HISTORY

In 1963, just prior to the announcement of System/360, Charles W. Bachman of the General Electric Company actively promoted Integrated Data Store (IDS) as some newfangled thing that managed data bases (as opposed to files). Someone thought that verbs should be included in COBOL (COmmon Business-Oriented Language) to facilitate management of the IDS network data model. An enterprising (and naive) IBM employee, who shall remain unnamed, thought this was a pretty good idea, so he dispatched a memo to the director of Programming Systems and asked whether or not such a facility was being considered in the programming support for the new product line (System/360).

What happened as the result of this relatively harmless question not only illustrates the long-standing nature of the data base controversy but also serves to introduce the subject of information bases. Xerox copiers were just beginning to appear in offices when this ill-fated memo was dispatched to the director of Programming Systems, and although the sender of the memo was careful to send a carbon copy (this is the historical section of this book) only to the subordinate who had brought IDS to his attention, a virtual information explosion occurred as copies of copies were made and distributed within IBM headquarters locations. All kinds of responses came from everywhere about the advisability of even considering such a harebrained scheme. (Remember, IBM was going to announce PL/1—Programming Language One—to replace COBOL.) The work generated was enough to swamp the small department that had had the temerity to raise the question in the first place.

It all finally came to an end when a corporate guru of something or other decreed: "We don't need this, we have ISAM (Indexed Sequential Access Method)." Subsequently, a number of internal projects came out of the closet as alternatives to IDS; some were even announced shortly after System/360 hit the streets. However, the task of explaining why ISAM was not really the same thing as IDS was too much for this early victim of xerography, and he retreated to the hallowed halls of a research facility before emerging to implement major on-line data bases for the corporation. This experience probably explains the normal reluctance to jump back into the data base fray today.

It is not important for us to know whether Ted Codd invented the relational model before Dick Pick invented the Pick operating system (although it has been a lively topic of controversy); however, it is interesting (and perhaps even important) to list some of the thoughts, theories, and facts about data "management" as they emerged within IBM in the 1960s. Please notice that I said "some," because the list is by no means all-inclusive. Figure 3.1 presents some of the "solutions" that were either available or being proposed to developers of "management information systems" during that period. The term "management information system" was itself relatively new, and it implied that data would be resident on direct access storage devices and would provide update (without destroying integrity), reporting (on a need-to-know basis), and some type of terminal access (without compromising security). While we have both refined and confused terminology considerably since that time, these remain the essential elements of a management information system. And, as we shall see, they remain the fundamental problems associated with distributed data bases.

Within IBM, the systems developer was confronted with the following array of data base "solutions."

The "facts" were that practically all data were entered into computer systems through punch cards and practically all files were sequential and on magnetic tape. When OS/360 was announced, it included a variety of "access methods" to support both direct access storage devices and terminals. Brief comments on these facts are as follows:

- Sequential files created an essentially batch orientation for updating of data bases, and both batch processing and sequential files remain a fact of life in most large IBM customer installations.

- Major IBM management information systems, and specifically the Advanced Administrative System (AAS), were implemented with heavy dependence on Basic Direct Access Method

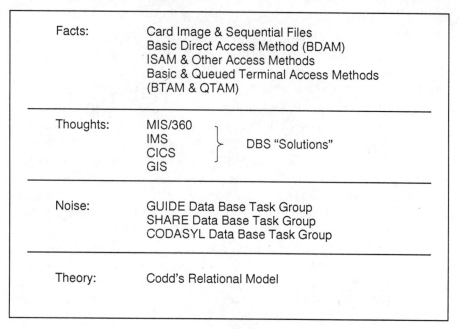

Figure 3.1 – IBM Data Base "Solutions"

Source: Killen & Associates, Inc.

· (BDAM) files. It is an embarrassing fact that such systems have been extremely resistant to replacement with IBM data base offerings for decades. In fact, I doubt whether substantial portions of AAS have ever been replaced with Information Management System (IMS).

• The corporate guru's ISAM attracted some IBM systems developers, with less than spectacular results. The first production test of a major IBM planning system based on ISAM ran all night on a dedicated large-scale mainframe and hardly made a dent in updating the file. At that point, an IBM systems programmer (who had not been consulted on the systems design) made a memorable observation: "Do you know what their problem is? They thought they knew what they were doing!"

• Both BTAM and Queued Telecommunication Access Method (QTAM) essentially left the responsibility for security of on-line files to the systems operator, who literally could access information to which even corporate vice presidents were not privy.

[This is essentially the condition most UNIX installations find themselves in today. The "systems administrator" (read operator) is responsible for security, and the "super users" (and assorted hackers) are free to wander through most of the systems at will. This is not acceptable in the commercial data processing environment.]

• The "facts" made it clear that some better means of managing data was necessary if management systems were to be developed.

IBM had numerous "thoughts" on what would be an effective answer to the management information systems implementation problem, but these thoughts did not originally address data base management as a formal discipline. Major and uncoordinated endeavors that were underway in the 1960s included the following:

• MIS/360 (yes, MIS stands for management information system) was an inverted file system very similar to what later came to be known as 4GLs (fourth-generation languages). It addressed the reporting and terminal query portions of an MIS with little attention to the update problem. File maintenance depended on "table cards" that were constantly changing, and separate systems were required for file updating. Years later, at another company, a corporate personnel "system" was "developed" using a still popular GL without any provision for updating the personnel files. However, in the 1960s there were those who felt that MIS/360 was pretty hot stuff. This prompted another systems programmer to make another memorable statement: "Those who think MIS/360 solves all the world's problems don't understand the data base problem."

- However, aside from MIS/360, there were other uncoordinated internal IBM efforts that came closer to addressing the data base problem. Confronted with a general lack of understanding of what the problem was, IBM shotgunned it by announcing three products: IMS, Customer Information Control System (CICS), and General Information System (GIS). This barrage was specifically addressed at quieting a lot of noise from IBM users about our old friend IDS. Fundamentally:

  - IMS addressed the data model (hierarchical) and updating problem.

  - CICS addressed the terminal accessing problem.

  - GIS addressed, to some degree, what we now know as the applications or report-generation problem. There were those who believed that COBOL could be replaced with GIS and remembered that IDS could potentially be integrated with CO-BOL.

- It was difficult for customers to accept the IMS, CICS, and GIS "solution" as an integrated solution to anything. All three evolved and continue to have their proponents to this day (although GIS has never proved popular in the general marketplace). Essentially, they were all aimed at stopping IDS and the network data model from becoming a standard, and in that they were successful.

The "noise" within IBM came from its user groups—GUIDE and SHARE. Charles W. Bachman, who came from a large IBM user (GE), was not averse to making his thinking on data bases known to other users and CODASYL (Conference on Data Systems Languages). Soon, both GUIDE and SHARE had established special task groups that started talking about schemas and subschemas and all sorts of stuff that most sequential file and FORTRAN (FORmula TRANslator) programmers had little time or inclination to even think about. IBM designated representatives to each of these task groups, and they continued to keep things stirred up within the IBM technical community. However, IBM's resistance to stan-

dards efforts has become legendary for good reason; business considerations ruled out any support for the network (CODASYL) model, and
IMS prevailed as IBM's DBMS of choice. Now, after more than two
decades, Bachman and IBM are business partners in trying to make SAA,
and specifically the Repository, work. More on this later.

During the 1960s, Dr. E. F. Codd of IBM was pursuing research in
data base theory relatively independently of users' current implementation
problems, the day-to-day infighting among those supporting various IBM
"solutions," or the power struggle developing around DBMS standards.
Dr. Codd was in the process of inventing the relational model. In June
1970, he published "A Relational Model for Large Shared Data Banks" in
the *Communications of the ACM*. With that, he jumped squarely into the
middle of the data base controversy, where he proved to be as single-
minded, persistent, and irascible as he is inventive. All these qualities
probably were essential. Not only was Codd responsible for conceiving
the relational model, he served as midwife during more than a decade of
labor that preceded IBM's announcement of DATABASE 2 (DB2) in
June 1983. That is enough to make anybody a trifle irritable.

This brief history brings us to the subject of data models, on which
I do not intend to spend a great deal of time. (A user who was inter-
viewed a few years ago stated: "I don't want to talk about data models—
the whole subject bores me.") However, to clear away the current and anticipated controversy on the subject, it is necessary to understand data models.

3.2   DATA MODELS

I will restrict this discussion as much as possible to the conceptual
or logical view of data models. Essentially, sequential files look like a
batch of sorted punch cards. The hierarchical model can be viewed as a
forest of tree structures, the network model as a collection of record types
and sets, and the relational model as a collection of tables (Figure 3.2).

I use the card "image" for sequential files because the systems
employing batch sequential processes were originally modeled after unit
record applications, and the management of these flat files remains essentially the same regardless of storage medium. Such management is characterized by programmer control (or responsibility) for establishing necessary procedures and programs for updating, file integrity, reporting, and
maintenance (including relatively trivial ad hoc reporting). However, there

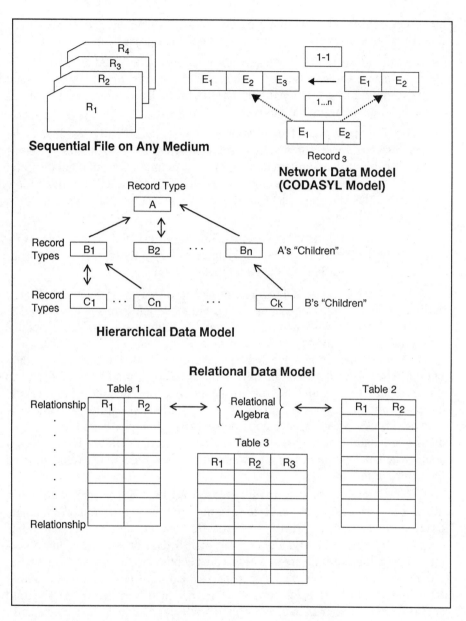

Figure 3.2 – General Data Model Schematics

Source: Killen & Associates, Inc.

are other reasons for maintaining the visual image of card decks even after they have disappeared in most advanced data processing facilities:

- Reading in a batch of unsorted records with fixed fields is really establishing a set of "tables." This is the essential conceptual model of a relational data base (admittedly without clean relationships between the fields).

- The fact that the relational model specifically excludes the requirement for a sorted set of tables and establishes a set of rules to assure mathematical correctness of the relationship between fields does not conceal the fact that the "intuitive" view of the relational data structure is essentially based on a deck of punch cards.

- More important, sequential files (sorting) and batch processing will play an important role in the distributed data base environment regardless of the data model of choice.

The network, or CODASYL, model is based on IDS, which I cited earlier. It is heavily dependent on pointers, which are anathema to Dr. Codd and the relational model. Conceptually, there is no reason why pointers could not be one-to-one, one-to-many, and many-to-many, but problems of implementation have led to the elimination of the many-to-many option. Therefore, the diagram in Figure 3.2 shows a solid-line pointer to illustrate one-to-one and a broken-line pointer to illustrate one-to-many; both are not permitted in current implementations. Despite its name, the network model presents enormous complexity of implementation in a true distributed data base environment. The very strength of the model disappears when the pointers become communications links and extend beyond the central data base.

The hierarchical data model epitomized by IMS suffers from a terminal case of brittleness, and this is not merely a question of old age. Even early in its life, IMS was not flexible enough to accommodate change very easily. Reorganizing a large IMS data base can become virtually impossible, and an organization can become frozen in place, a veritable prisoner of its DBMS. Major reorganizations have occurred within IBM that would have been impossible if IBM had been firmly locked into an IMS data base. IMS will be around for a long time, primarily because a significant number of major IBM customers have become trapped. IMS is not suitable for implementing distributed data bases for the following reasons:

- The aforementioned concerns about flexibility effectively rule IMS out for anything except large central data bases.

- It is difficult to use and requires a staff of data base administrators (no matter what their job titles are) that seems to increase along with data base size.

- The IMS system itself is so large that it cannot possibly run on a distributed processor. This effectively rules out locating the processing close to the transaction point, which is where transactions should be processed.

- And, the performance of IMS is not all that great either. The fact that IMS is now being touted as a high-performance system should not obscure the fact that it has sold more large-scale mainframes than even IBM had reason to believe possible, and it suffers when compared with systems (such as IDMS) that employ the network model. Only when compared with DB2 can IMS be classified a high-performance system—which brings us to the relational model.

The relational model provides a formal and mathematically correct means of addressing the management of data bases. We all have Dr. Codd to thank for that, and the industry did so by awarding him the ACM Turing Award in 1981. We also extend to Dr. Codd the courtesy of letting him define what a relational DBMS is, and I defend his right to classify nonconforming systems as "semi-relational," "relational-like," or any other terminology he chooses. The relational data model will be described in more detail later because it will play an essential role in the distributed data base environment. IBM's SAA depends heavily on it, and it is difficult to identify any other single invention on which IBM has had so much at stake. If we find that Dr. Codd's creation is less than perfect, it will not diminish its importance to IBM's business strategy.

Before proceeding with a brief description of the relational model, I must mention, even more briefly, some other developments in the data model area. This is provided primarily as background information, and I make no pretense of technically describing the data models.

The entity-relationship model is based on a view of the real world which consists of a set of basic objects (entities) and the relationships among those objects. The model was developed to facilitate data base design by providing a means of specifying an overall logical structure for an enterprise data base. All the data models in Figure 3.2 could be depicted using entity-relationship (E-R) diagrams, thus providing an "enterprise scheme" that might prove extremely beneficial (and even essential) in determining the shared use of data by various applications systems within the enterprise. The importance of the entity-relationship model becomes apparent when dealing with the relational model in a distributed environment. Its use will be discussed later. (Since the long-awaited Repository was announced in 1989, E-R diagrams probably will become as familiar as programming flow charts used to be.)

The set theoretic data model was developed with the thought that users should be able to take any conceptual view of data they wanted and that hardware and software implementation could make this possible with acceptable performance. While this is intuitively attractive, any implementation compromises the relational model (or certainly its effective use in the distributed environment).

The surrogate data model was based on full text indices and, to the best of my knowledge, has never been formalized in terms of tying text to structured data bases. I mention this only because structured data, text, and images need to be treated in some reasonably consistent fashion. Numerous software packages that begin to address this problem are currently available for personal computers. The Apple HyperCard is a step toward an area I prefer to think of as "information base" management. It is an area of extreme importance, but it is beyond the scope of this book.

3.3   THE RELATIONAL MODEL

For our purposes, I will generally describe the relational model as it was presented by Dr. Codd in his ACM Turing Award lecture. I will avoid a detailed definition, but the presentation should suffice to distinguish what is *not* a relational data base system.

Since the relational model represents data in tabular form, there have been those who questioned using the term "relational" rather than "tabular." Dr. Codd is more than equal to the task of defending the nomenclature. He has stated that the term "relational" was specifically selected to counter the popular opinion: (1) that a relationship between two or more objects had to be represented by a linked structure, and (2) that tables were considered a lower level of abstraction than relations because tables imply that positional addressing is inherent and do not convey the information that a table is independent of row order (relational tables are not key sorted).

Codd's objectives in defining the relational model were:

(1) To achieve data independence by defining a clear boundary between the logical and physical aspects of data base management

(2) To provide a simple structure that could be easily understood (and used) by end users, programmers, and data base administrators

(3) To introduce high-level language concepts to facilitate set processing and relieve users of the data base from being concerned with handling individual records when multiple sets are processed

Any data model consists of three components: (1) a defined set of data structure types; (2) a collection of operators or rules of inference to derive, modify, or retrieve data from the defined structure types; and (3) a general set of integrity rules that implicitly or explicitly defines a set of consistent data base states, or changes of state, or both. These three components are outlined in Figure 3.3.

As mentioned previously, the relational model consists of tables of fields (elements), rows, and columns. The fields can be either key fields or nonkey fields. Despite the various ways in which tables can be structured, the structures can easily be visualized and represented. (I will avoid defining the terminology, not because it cannot be easily explained, but because other components of the model are more difficult and it is not necessary to have a detailed explanation to make my point.) The essential points about the structure of the relational model are:

- It is flexible.
- It is easy to visualize and use.
- It can improve productivity (Codd's Turing lecture was titled "Relational Data Base: A Practical Foundation for Productivity") by providing end users with direct access to information stored in computers and by making applications programs easier to develop.

The relational algebra naturally contributes to this improved productivity by providing the basic set processing operators that Codd envisioned in his original objectives. One of Codd's primary purposes in specifying the relational algebra was to avoid using iterative or recursive statements when defining languages that implement the relational algebra. (If you want a data base system classified as "nonrelational," include IFs and/or DOs in the query language.) Both string-oriented languages, such as Standard Query Language (SQL), and two-dimensional, screen-oriented languages, such as QUBE, can support the full relational algebra (three-val-

Data Structure Types

Tables structured and defined by:
records, fields, domains, relations, tables, attributes,
elements, degree, cardinality, binary relations,
"N-ary" relations, "N-tuples," candidate keys,
and primary keys.

Set (Table) Processing Capability

The *Relational Algebra* consisting of basic operators:
SELECT, PROJECT, and JOIN.

General Integrity Rules

The five Normal Forms for relational data bases:

First Normal Form: all occurrences of a record type must
contain the same number of fields.

Second Normal Form: a nonkey field must not contain
a fact about a subset of the key field.

Third Normal Form: a nonkey field must not contain
a fact about another nonkey field.

Fourth Normal Form: must conform to Third Normal Form
and cannot contain two or more independent facts
about an entity.

Fifth Normal Form: covers cases where information can
be reconstructed from smaller pieces that can be
maintained with less redundancy.

Figure 3.3 – The Relational Model

ued predicate logic with a single kind of rule). Presently, SQL is IBM's obvious choice for SAA.

Some subtle (and some not so subtle) problems are associated with the building of languages to support what Codd calls "relational processing." Since languages are one of the most important elements of SAA and ease of use, it is desirable to have some idea of exactly what Dr. Codd thinks about the subject. The following are some of his thoughts.

- First of all, to be considered relational a data base management system must have a data sublanguage that at least supports the relational processing capability by performing the transformations specified by SELECT, PROJECT, and unrestricted JOIN, without resorting to commands for iteration and recursion. The "unrestricted JOIN" refers to the possibility that some language implementations might restrict the JOIN operator by having to have attributes with the same name or a predefined access path. (I will discuss some important and unfortunate performance consequences of the "unrestricted JOIN" later.)

- Codd recommends that any DBMS that does not support relational processing be classified as "nonrelational," but suggests that a DBMS that supports tables without user-visible navigation links between the tables might be classified as "tabular."

- While a relational sublanguage need not be embedded within a host language because relational data base systems do not need a query language that requires iteration, it is usually desirable to embed them in commercial DBMSs. Early implementations (System R and INGRES) included sublanguages for both host languages and terminal. These "double-mode" languages are obviously essential in today's environment (and in SAA), and Codd embraced them immediately and established another classification for them—"uniform relational." This leaves relational sublanguages that do not support both modes as "non-uniform relational."

- It is obviously difficult to implement a "uniform-relational" system because the relational processing capability must be interfaced with a host language that is oriented toward processing one record at a time. The answer is to derive a relation in the form of a file that can be read by the host language, and then:

- Either leave the delivery of the records to the host language file system, or

- Have the data sublanguage keep control of record delivery and provide record-by-record access to the program written in the host language.

• In his 1981 Turing Award lecture, Codd went to some length to assure us that the second case does not violate the relational definition: "It is important to note that in advancing a cursor over a derived relation, the programmer is not engaging in navigation to some target area. The derived relation is itself the target data!"

• Since 1981, two significant events have occurred which may affect the purity of relational processing and its associated languages: (1) the personal computer has emerged as a new standard of ease of use, and (2) IBM has adopted a dual data base strategy.

• While the personal computer has certainly given impetus to set processing and the relational model, it is also important to recognize that an enormous number of programmers and end users have been exposed to navigating through the trees (hierarchy) of PC- (or MS-) DOS, and "windowing" adds another dimension to the tabular representation of data. Combined with IBM's dual data base strategy, languages and user interfaces will considerably strain IBM's abilities to integrate relational data base management systems under the SAA umbrella effectively enough to satisfy the relational purists.

The problems associated with effective implementation are primarily those of performance. Despite claims to the contrary, the unrestricted JOIN is an intrinsic performance problem with relational processing. IBM did not announce a relational DBMS before 1983 primarily because acceptable performance could not be achieved. (And when IBM is concerned about performance, everyone should listen.) As System R struggled through its performance problems, someone reportedly said: "Being better than awful can still be pretty bad." I should also point out that even the best optimization will not achieve satisfactory performance in certain environments.

When making what would be relatively simple queries against a sequential file (or table), a relational data base system may be confronted with joining two tables. This potentially results in having to examine the first row of the first table against each row of the second table until the second table is exhausted, then proceeding serially through each row of the first table with the same procedure. The entire second table will be serially searched as many times as there are rows in the first table.

Effectively, this means that as the number of rows being processed with a natural (unrestricted) JOIN increases, the number of potential accesses to storage (the data base) increases approximately twice as fast. Sequential tables can expand enormously in size with relatively little penalty if they employ a simple binary search. The linking, indexing, and navigation that Codd deplores also permit both hierarchical and network data bases to grow without the risk of this inherent performance problem.

The performance problems of the relational model are legendary, and finding solutions for them has been severely challenging to computer scientists. As recently as 1981, when Codd was delivering his ACM Turing Award lecture, the *IBM Systems Journal* (G. Sandberg, Volume 20, No. 1, 1981) published the following:

- "The method of operation for a join is very time consuming and expensive if implemented directly as described. That has been a criticism of relational systems since the beginning. However, improved techniques in areas of optimization and indexing are developing. . . . Thus, in the JOIN operation previously discussed, if there were an index on a column in the second table, only the index might have to be searched. . . . Further, if there were also an index on a column in the first table, the search for equal values could be performed entirely in the indexes. The data base system may also keep statistics about actual or intended usage, in order to optimize the search order internally. It now seems that improved optimization methods are sufficiently developed to make possible large-scale relational *testing* [my emphasis]."

- I should point out that much of this optimization, insofar as it addresses queries, must take place during execution. The theory is that access to direct access storage is slow; therefore, lots of computer power is available for optimization. This is true, but large data bases are shared, and extensive optimization time detracts from the overall performance of the system. In addition, keeping "statistics" can contribute so much to systems overhead that it is not practical in operational environments.

- Since IBM released DB2 to the world approximately two years after the article in the *IBM Systems Journal*, substantial "testing" of large-scale relational data base systems is probably currently going on in the user community.

In the meantime, Dr. Codd, Chris Date, and Sharon Weinberg have left the internal IBM data base wars to fight in the streets. In some ways The Relational Institute performs some very useful services in keeping the peddlers of "relational-like" systems reasonably honest. An official "Codd-Date" stamp on a relational product may be helpful to users confronted with the relational craze in the marketplace. However, when the subject of performance comes up, the staff of this supposedly objective "institute" behaves like a paranoid ostrich that takes its head out of the sand long enough to strike out in all directions against anything in sight. In the late 1980s, the trade press published the following:

- The usually thorough Dr. Codd published an oversimplified analysis on the subject of relational performance which essentially said that intelligent implementation of relational data base management systems was all that was necessary. He gratuitously reminded implementors that the solution was "called optimization."

- Mr. Date published an article that stated: "The relational performance myth is finally debunked once and for all. It is a milestone in data base history" ("Debunking the Myth of Relational Systems," *Computerworld*, March 30, 1987). (He reached this conclusion by comparing the transaction rates on a single Tandem relational system test against those achieved by IMS on an IBM system, which is something like comparing lemons and tomatoes.)

- Ms. Weinberg is president of the Codd and Date Consulting Group, an offshoot of The Relational Institute. She is reported to have publicly attacked a highly publicized test in which DB2 achieved only 30 percent of the equally highly publicized transaction rates achieved in another test. Ms. Weinberg stated that the test was "unfair," apparently without any detailed knowledge of how it was conducted. This is the type of objectivity that the "consulting" profession can ill afford.

Considerable discussion of the relational model has been necessary because it will have a key role to play in a distributed data base environment. However, as we proceed toward this environment, it is wise to remember that the relational model is a resource hog of both processing power and disk storage. In a distributed environment, these performance characteristics become even more important. We need as much information as we can get as customers "test" the applications limits of relational data base systems. Denying that there is a problem does little to solve it— quite the contrary.

4

Distributed Data Base Management

Suddenly it seems that everyone is talking about distributed data bases. In fact, there has even been talk that 1989 was the "year of distributed data bases." One more realistic analyst observed that it might more properly be classified as the year we started planning for distributed data bases. I believe that most customers were not even ready to start planning for distributed data bases in 1989. In any case, before planning starts, the problems should be clearly understood, and most vendors have been inclined to obscure the problems with either wishful thinking or partial solutions.

Before presenting the problems of distributed data base management, I should point out that the current interest in distributed data bases is prompted primarily by a perceived upheaval in the hardware processing hierarchy. From a straight hardware point of view, classic economies of scale have been seriously disrupted. Grosch's law, which stated that the cost of an executed machine instruction was inversely proportional to the square of the size of the machine, seems to have been destroyed by minicomputers and microprocessors. The acceptance of MIPS (million instructions per second) as a performance measure leads to the illusion that every desktop has the power of a large mainframe of just a few years ago. While this may be valid for certain functions, such as information editing and display (see Figure 2.4), the economics of both minicomputers and microprocessors for effective work against large data bases is misleading at best and downright dangerous in the context of distributed data bases.

When data base systems were first developed, computer systems had a common problem that should be remembered. All too often the hardware would be installed and the software for a system would be developed before the data to support the application were available. Today, there is a corporate struggle for data, which is being encouraged by hardware vendors at various levels (Figure 4.1). The danger today is that the distribution of data will occur before we have the ability to manage those data.

4.1 THE PROBLEMS

Three fundamental problems have been identified with respect to the management of distributed data bases:

(1) Data base synchronization refers to the fact that even when data are valid, different versions may exist, which can create problems. The problems are primarily related to time. One of the primary advantages of centralized data bases is that everyone is working against the same version at any given time. When data bases are distributed over a network, ensuring synchronization is a nontrivial problem.

(2) Data base integrity is concerned primarily with the updating of data bases and the potential for contamination and/or loss of data. All the lessons learned about data base management are important in this regard. The need for data base administrators becomes apparent whenever data are shared (much less distributed). Even in the early work on structured methodologies, programming project teams needed "librarians" to assure the integrity of program libraries. All the lessons learned the hard way on mainframes probably will have to be relearned as data bases are distributed. While it may be possible to have an unattended departmental processor from an operational point of view, any significant data bases distributed to that level will require some form of local data base administration. And at the level of personal computers, even the sharing and exchange of word processing documents is making such fundamental lessons as backup and update control apparent. In addition, the personal computer has provided a wonderful tool for deliberate mischief directed against data bases. Problems of data base integrity increase enormously in a network environment.

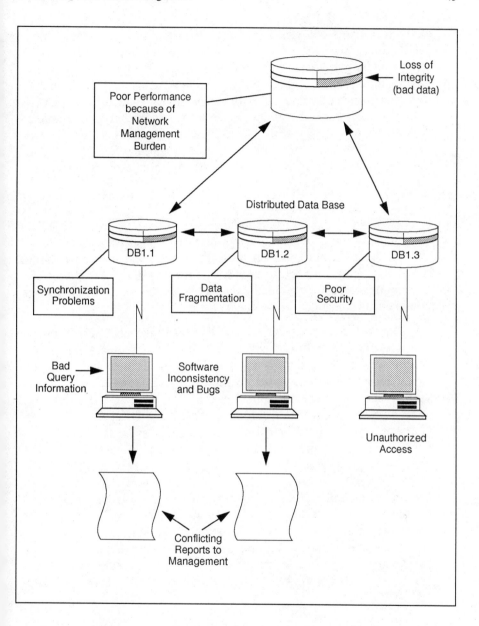

Figure 4.1 – Problems in Information Quality

Source: Killen & Associates, Inc.

(3)   Security is concerned primarily with access to data. It is obviously more secure to keep money in a bank than it is to stuff it away under everyone's mattress, and one could make a close analogy to the security problem in a distributed data base environment. Even with considerable effort by knowledgeable security specialists at large mainframe installations, teenage hackers have been able to penetrate supposedly secure data bases and distribute credit card numbers on computer bulletin boards. Personal, physical, and technical security problems increase dramatically as data bases are distributed.

It is important to recognize that all three of the above problems remain unresolved in existing or announced systems and are classified by computer scientists as "requiring more research." Hardware or software vendors who claim to have solved these three technical problems should be viewed as highly suspect. But even giving them the benefit of the doubt, we must say that distributed data bases still have two problems that will remain even if the technical problems are solved.

(1)   Information quality in a fully distributed data base environment will be exceptionally difficult to maintain. The problem is that the processing of these distributed data bases at the personal computer level leads to conflicting information. This is likely because not all individuals will understand the data they are dealing with, and they will not all process it in a similar fashion (either because of dissimilar tools or because of their use of these tools). It is also true that individual users are not trained as systems personnel, and, that the use of either spreadsheet packages or data base systems on PCs can be error-prone. The current emphasis on pretty reports has diverted attention from the substantive quality of the information being conveyed. This is an extremely critical issue in determining whether or not data bases should even be distributed. As one information systems executive stated: "I think every personal computer should be hardwired to produce a statement on every printed report which says: THIS REPORT WAS NOT PREPARED BY THE MIS DEPARTMENT."

(2)   Performance in terms of hardware-software-service overhead costs to solve the technical problems associated with distributed data base management may be so bad that even if the technical problems can be solved, any economic justification will disappear. The

burden and cost of systems software, communications, and storage of replicated data bases are potentially enormous. The network may literally talk itself to death with messages to keep everything in sync and secure, much less to avoid the "deadly embrace" of grid-locked data sets.

Considering the potential problems of information quality (Figure 4.1), it is little wonder that distributed data base management has remained a subject of academic study and terminological erosion characterized by changing definitions to fit capability. If there are so many problems, why worry about distributed data base management at all? Unfortunately, there are good reasons to worry about these problems because there are pressing needs for effective management of distributed data bases.

4.2   THE NEED FOR DISTRIBUTED DATA BASE MANAGEMENT

The academic view of the trade-offs in distributing data bases is as follows:

- The advantages of distributing data bases are the sharing of data, reliability and availability, and the "speedup" of query processing.
- The disadvantages are software development cost, greater potential bugs, and increased processing overhead.
- The simple statement "greater potential bugs" was explained in a recently published book to mean the following: "Since the sites that comprise the distributed system operate in parallel, it is harder to ensure the correctness of algorithms. The potential exists for extremely subtle bugs. The art of constructing distributed algorithms remains an active and important area of research."

Essentially, the academic view seems to be that distributed data base management systems will be more costly to implement, may not work, and will have higher operational costs. The offsetting benefits would hardly seem worth the time and trouble. This has caused many to question the circumstances and business justification for even attempting to develop systems that are obviously beyond practical implementation in today's world.

One level removed from the academic environment, those responsible for the actual implementation of computer/communications networks see the following advantages in distributing data (Figure 4.2):

- Processing costs are perceived to decrease.
- Ease of use improves.
- The placement of data at local sites can reduce the amount of data transferred among network computers and reduce communications costs.
- Local access to these data can reduce response time.
- With replicated data bases, reliability can be increased by having data located at more than one site.
- The provision for local storage gives users more control over data, and, hopefully, this will result in better-quality data because users will be made responsible for data accuracy.

One author facetiously stated that the challenge of the technical problems was also being used to justify the distribution of data. While he did not seriously recommend that this "climb the mountain because it is there" philosophy be used for actual justification, he did state that "making it work" can be the motivation of some technicians. It is wise to remember this.

Once again, when the technical challenges are analyzed, the cost justification becomes quite complex—and substantial risk is involved in implementing distributed data bases.

I am inclined to take a more pragmatic view of the need. The need for distributed data base management has become critical because data bases are being distributed and/or developed on a decentralized basis, regardless of whether we have the ability to manage them. The success of minicomputers and personal computers has turned the scholarly pursuit of interesting problems associated with distributed data bases into a matter of utmost priority. Decentralized data bases do not become manageable when they are connected—quite the contrary. Increased exchange of data across processing levels (Figure 4.1) to take advantage of perceived advantages at those processing levels (Figure 4.2) can have a disastrous (and potentially catastrophic) impact on the quality of data, information, and corporate performance. The problems of distributed data base management should be of more than academic interest, but all too frequently they are ignored in the pursuit of individual vendors' partial solutions, which only reinforce the need for distributed data base management.

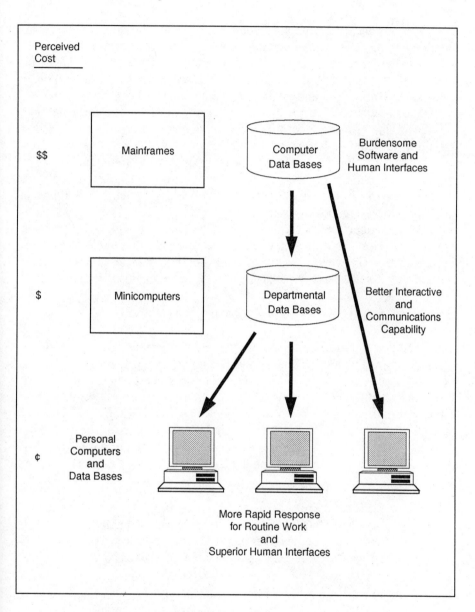

Figure 4.2 – Perceived Advantages of Distribution

Source: Killen & Associates, Inc.

Besides the fact that data are already being distributed over computer/communications networks in a chaotic fashion, there are other reasons to believe that solving the technical problems associated with distributed data base management should be viewed with increased urgency. Data, information, and knowledge are being integrated in computer/communications networks before they are understood or even clearly defined. It is becoming increasingly difficult to distinguish among the three, but one thing is certain—both information and knowledge are relatively useless unless they are supported by meaningful data of high quality. (The problems of data, information, and knowledge integration will be explained briefly in the next chapter of this book.) The hard technology in terms of processing power (microprocessors), high-speed integrated communications [fiber optics and ISDN (Integrated Services Digital Network)], and storage (optical memories) is becoming available to support this integration. However, the promise of the "information age" will never be realized without effective management of the resulting integrated system.

4.3   THE "SOLUTIONS" AND THE REALITY

The fact that the problems associated with distributed data base management are not generally understood and/or are being ignored has led to a broad range of "solutions." This, in turn, raises questions about the definition of a distributed data base. The solutions range from simple micromainframe links (which also present problems of definition) to a set of 12 rules that parallel Codd's 12 rules for the relational model. The following is a very brief summary of a more detailed definition presented by Chris Date of The Relational Institute and the Codd and Date Consulting Group.

- Rule 1: Local Autonomy, which means:
    - Data are locally owned and managed with local accountability. Even Date admits that, in practical applications, Rule 1 is not totally achievable and suggests that it can be more accurately stated as "sites should be autonomous to the maximum extent possible."

    - Local operations should remain purely local, and users should not be penalized for their participation in the distributed system.

    - No one site should depend on another site for its successful functioning.

- Rule 2: No Reliance on a Central Site, which means that the following functions must all be distributed: dictionary management, query processing, concurrency control, and recovery control.

- Rule 3: Continuous Operation, which is viewed as an objective, since there are instances in which shutdown is inevitable. Specifically, Date is referring to cases where additional sites are being incorporated in the network or the DBMS itself is being upgraded to a new release. The network should not have to be brought down to accomplish these.

- Rule 4: Location Independence, which is key to the concept of distributed data base management. Users should not have to know where data are physically stored and should be able to perform tasks (at least logically) as if the data were all stored at their own site.

- Rule 5: Fragmentation Independence, which requires that a given relation can be divided into pieces or "fragments" for physical storage purposes. Fragmentation of relations may be accomplished either horizontally or vertically, based on the relational operations of restriction and projection, respectively, and may be reconstructed using union and join operations. (Date notes that ease of fragmentation and reconstruction are "two of the many reasons why distributed systems must be relational"—and he is right about that!)

- Rule 6: Replication Independence, which requires that a given relation (or fragment of a relation) can be represented at the physical level by many distinct stored copies or replicas at many distinct sites. (One of the biggest arguments that IBM used in the 1970s against distributed processing was that data bases had to be duplicated.)

- Rule 7: Distributed Query Processing, which essentially means that the process of optimization that is so critical to relational performance becomes even more complex. (Date points out that the selection of a good query strategy is "crucial"—he is right, but that places a lot of responsibility (or blame) on the implementors.)

- Rule 8: Distributed Transaction Management, which implies that the equally critical considerations of recovery control and concurrency control (at the heart of the integrity and synchronization problems) become more complex. As Date puts it: "each requires extended treatment in the distributed environment." Date has detailed knowledge of the problems that must be addressed in this environment. He states:

– "Local autonomy states that each site must be responsible for lock management of its own local data . . . as a result, global deadlock is possible" (the deadly embrace).

– "The problem is that no site can detect it, using only information to other sites."

– Therefore, to detect such deadlocks, "sites must send some of their internal information to other sites."

– However, since the definition presented prescribes that there "should not be any central 'deadlock detector' site to which all sites send such information . . . the system should provide some kind of distributed deadlock detection mechanism."

– Returning to reality, Rule 8 concludes: "Alternatively, given that the global deadlock detection is liable to be expensive (because of the additional message traffic it entails), it may be preferable to use some kind of time-out mechanism to prevent deadlocks from occurring in the first place." The only conclusion one can draw about Rule 8 is that "some kind of" solution is required for a very real implementation problem of the Date definition of distributed data base management.

• Rule 9: Hardware Independence, which is essentially what it says.

• Rule 10: Operating System Independence, which is not essentially what it says because "from a commercial point of view" the definition suggests a minimum. Not surprisingly, this minimum set includes "IBM's MVS/XA (Multiple Virtual Storage/Extended Architecture), VM/CMS (Virtual Memory/CMS), Digital Equipment's VAX/VMS, UNIX in various flavors, and PC-DOS."

• Rule 11: Network Independence, which is comparable to Rule 10 in its meaning since it specifies the most commonly used network architectures as a base, once again concentrating on IBM's SNA and Digital Equipment's DECnet.

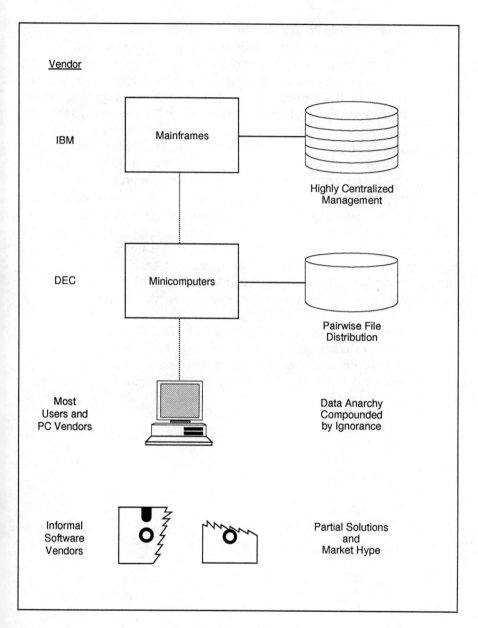

Figure 4.3 – Where Things Stand

Source: Killen & Associates, Inc.

- Rule 12: DBMS Independence, which is getting down to the "it would be nice if those different data base systems could all participate somehow in a distributed system" type of rule which is, once again, no sooner postulated than it is qualified out of existence. Date's 12 rules were no sooner presented than they started to draw the fire of more practical souls who questioned such fundamental concepts as local autonomy and the need for distributed data bases. So, in summary, there is no clear definition of distributed data bases, and there are implementation problems that are recognized even among their strongest proponents.

The reality of the situation is that vendors and consultants are each proposing definitions and "solutions" that are most closely associated with their particular products, theories, interests, and understanding. Figure 4.3 presents a current and humble assessment of where things stand. It is an environment of chaos and danger for users, and their initial reaction is often to return to the protective fold of you-know-who or to stand perfectly still like a deer in a spotlight, even when the danger moves ever closer.

It is an environment well suited for IBM, and SAA may even be on the right track in addressing some of the distributed data base problems and the needs of its users. We will look at IBM's awareness of and role in the distributed data base wars later in this book, but first, let us stand back and take a look at the "information age."

5

The "Information Age"

At the dawn of the industrial revolution, there was little concern about what would happen to the craftsmen or laborers who might be replaced by factories and mechanization. New goods, products, and services were clearly the output of that revolution, and it could be argued that everyone's quality of life would be improved substantially by industrialization. Only the distribution of this new wealth was a subject for debate and political revolution.

The age of mass production that followed certainly caused some concern as long hours and low pay became the subject of negotiations between management and labor. There was even talk of man becoming the slave of the assembly line (machine). And there was much debate concerning whether shorter working hours would lead to the pursuit of cultural activities or merely produce "idle hands" with which the devil could play.

The alarming thing about the heralded "information age" is that it has no definable product, nor is there serious debate or concern about its potential consequences. The information age has demonstrated great potential for bootstrapping itself by obscuring the distinctions between data, information, and knowledge (to say nothing of propaganda and advertising) and by overwhelming the reasoned analyses of prophets, "gurus," financial analysts, vendors (hardware, software, and communications), consultants, academicians, forecasters, and authors—all armed with the tools of the information age. With that modest introduction, I shall now define data, information, and knowledge.

53

5.1   DATA, INFORMATION, AND KNOWLEDGE

Data, information, and knowledge are not clearly understood, nor is their complex interaction in systems that are being built today.

Fritz Machlup, an economist, did the best work here. In his essay, "Semantic Quirks in Studies of Information," published in *The Study of Information: Interdisciplinary Messages*, edited by the late Fritz Machlup and Una Mansfield (John Wiley and Sons, Inc., 1983), Machlup defined these terms. The book is a collection of essays that are organized under the following major disciplines: cognitive science, computer and information science, artificial intelligence, linguistics, library and information science, cybernetics, information theory, mathematical system theory, and general system theory. I do not expect any belabored MIS director, chief information officer, or business/computer science student to fully understand all these disciplines, but I believe he or she should know how important these disciplines will be in the information age and what potential impact they will have on the systems he or she will be developing.

Machlup is credited with the "first scholarly pronouncement on the 'Information Economy' in 1962." While he was an economist rather than a linguist, he thought it important to include his own essay, which "quibbles" about the semantic quirks inherent in *The Study of Information*. His definitions of data, information, and knowledge are quite clear and to the point.

After considerable discussion of the use and misuse of the term "data" (partially because of "linguistic ignorance," according to Machlup), he proceeds to wrap up the definition quite neatly:

> This semantic muddle, however, need not cause any serious trouble, because arguments in which data, whatever they are, play a central role are relatively simple: Data entry, data storage, data retrieval, data processing, data services, and all the rest refer simply to things fed into a computer. These things, now data from the point of view of the programmers, operators, and users of the computer, need not be data in any other sense.

Machlup then points out that:

> Drafts of a manuscript for a learned monograph (or mystery story, for that matter) may have been typed into a computer; or the subject index for a test book; a bibliography of writings on the history of French paint-

ing; detailed statistics of the gross national income of the United States from 1940 to 1980; expert knowledge for the diagnosis of diseases of various kinds; graphs and images of all sorts; or what not.

He continues that regardless of whether they are pieces of fragmented information (football scores from CompuServe) or elaborate "compendia of systematic knowledge in some discipline," to computer users they are all data stored and retrieved.

He concludes that there is no hope of connecting data to its original roots in Latin where data are the "givens" and datum is the "given." The word "data" has been preempted and distorted by the computer types, and he is content to let them have it. However, he is not prepared to have "information" suffer the same fate.

Machlup deplores the appropriation of the word "information" as specific "designata," different from the common meanings. He points out that the word does remain in the dictionary and that we have no right to ignore it. The dictionary defines the verb "inform" as: "To impart knowledge of some particular fact or occurrence to; to tell (one) something." And, the noun "information" means: "That of which one is apprised or told; intelligence, news." He goes on to state: "any meanings other than (1) the telling of something or (2) that which is being told are either analogies and metaphors or concoctions resulting from the condoned appropriation of a word for something that had not been meant by earlier users."

The use and misuse of the word "information" among the various disciplines that are covered in *The Study of Information* is then explored. The major points are as follows:

- Scientists tend to use "observation" and "information" as equivalent terms. Machlup points out that information requires at least two persons—one who tells (by speaking, writing, imprinting, pointing, signaling) and one who listens, reads, or watches—and that information is just a metaphor for observation. (Since most scientific observation is directed toward the physical environment, it could be that God is trying to tell us something, but I reject anthropomorphism of either God or machines.)

- The restricted use of "information" as supporting decisions and actions by reducing uncertainty differs from the common usage of the word, and Machlup rather gently points out that information can, in fact, increase uncertainty.

- The term "information" has become an all-purpose weasel word in describing the functioning of the nervous system, but while Machlup deplores the general degeneration of proper usage, he admits it is difficult to avoid the use of this term in certain contexts. (For example, tactile sensations from mechanical stimulation could be a piece of information encoded by receptors and decoded by neurons.

- The use of "information" in describing the genetic system has become prevalent since the discovery of the genetic code, which has a kind of written language. It is difficult to describe this language without reverting to the fact that the genetic system "could convey more than 300,000,000 words of written prose" in a reference manual for building a human. And, the associated terminology, such as "stored," "imprinted," "copying," "transcript," and "translation," is hard to avoid. Machlup only wonders whether extending the analogy will lead to fuzzy distinctions between content and the actual physical representations of information.

- "The fundamental notion of information is the same in all social sciences (society, polity, and economy)." Machlup warns that the primary problem associated with the social sciences view of information is that there is a tendency to assume that there is "social information (or knowledge)," which implies that the whole has a mind of its own. (This is an especially dangerous concept as we approach the "information age," and the danger exists whether there is complete freedom of information flow or whether it is restricted in order to control this imaginary mind.)

Machlup then gets to the heart of the matter with which we are most concerned—the use of the term "information" in man-made systems. His conclusions are as follows:

- Going back to Norbert Wiener's *Cybernetics* (MIT Press, 1948), he finds the term "feedback" defined as "the chain of transmission and return of information" along with the observation that there are "feedback chains in which no human element intervenes." Machlup concludes that the definition does little harm as long as we clearly understand that the term (information) is being used as a metaphor.

- He is not so lenient with Claude Shannon (known as the founder of information theory) and his development of information theory as it relates to the essential signal processing which is at the heart of today's computer/communications networks. He concludes that when information theorists speak of information, it is a "sad misuse of language."

- Machlup firmly states that the use of the word "information" "where only observation and analysis are involved, is just confusion," and that those who believe that the observation of physical reality or "consultation" of data "tells" us anything have "misunderstood the basic lessons of methodology."

Aside from making a lot of chief information officers feel even more unsure of exactly what they are supposed to be doing, does all of this have any significance? It does. When you define your terms clearly, you eliminate confusion. Knowledge and information are very different things; the primary distinctions between them are as follows:

- Information is piecemeal, fragmented, and particular; knowledge is structured, coherent, and frequently universal.

- Information is timely, transitory, and perhaps even ephemeral; knowledge is of enduring significance.

- Information is a flow of messages; knowledge is the stock that results from this flow of messages.

- Machlup also makes the following observations:

  - Information is acquired by being told; knowledge can be acquired by thinking.

  - Therefore, new knowledge can be acquired without new information being received.

It is very convenient to adopt what are essentially Fritz Machlup's definitions of data, information, and knowledge (Figure 5.1).

- Everything stored in a computer system is considered data. Even messages (electronic mail, voice recordings, or full video for that matter) are treated as data within the system. This implies that they should be managed just as are "normal" accounting and statistical data.

- Information is revealed when a human "tells" something by "speaking, writing, imprinting, pointing, signaling (such as sticking out one's tongue)." By my definition, receiving an electronic

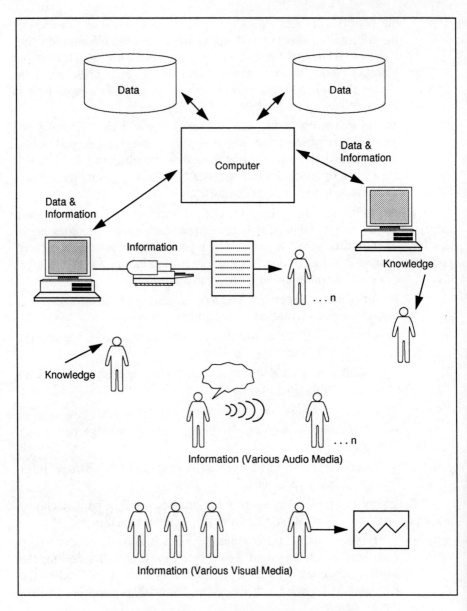

Figure 5.1 – Data, Information, and Knowledge,
Communication and Storage

Source: Killen & Associates, Inc.

message at a computer terminal provides information, but browsing through United States census data (or intercepting someone else's mail) does not, although information may be generated based on those data. Currently, most information in a business environment continues to be communicated and stored on paper —enormous, ever-increasing quantities of paper. (Any information of significance from meetings, telephone conversations, etc., is normally recorded on paper.)

- Today, practically all *knowledge* is stored in human brains. Based on the individual's knowledge, information may be ignored, screened, interpreted, classified, discarded (forgotten), or retained as part of the knowledge base, or it may trigger an immediate response like a punch in the nose or a kiss on the cheek. The exact same information may trigger all these responses in any group of individuals or in the same individual under different circumstances. Direct cause and effect of information (being told) doesn't work very well between human beings. You must deal with probabilities in the social "sciences" at a much higher level than you do in quantum mechanics. "Knowledge bases" will continue to reside in human heads, and computer programs of any genre, regardless of the number of "if statements," should be considered data when they are resident on a computer network and should be managed as such.

None of the latter-day prophets of the "information age"—among whom we include Alvin Toffler (author of *Future Shock*) and John Naisbitt (author of *Megatrends*)—are either mentioned or cited by the 41 contributors to *The Study of Information: Interdisciplinary Messages*. While it is not surprising that these gentlemen are excluded from any serious study of information, it is worth noting that their opinions have helped to form the expectations that many of our leaders have for computer/communications technology. The gap between these expectations and reality can be quite substantial—especially when the basic assumption seems to be that all information has value, and emphasis is placed on form rather than content.

5.2 THE PROPHETS

The seed of the information age was planted by IBM around 1960. For data processing (as opposed to computational) applications, IBM presented its major customers with a scenario, which can be paraphrased as follows:

> "Up to now you have used computers to save money,
> now you should start using computers to make money."

Implicit in this statement is the promise that data processing can create wealth and have a positive impact on the "bottomline" not merely by saving money used for clerical and accounting personnel (which never really happened anyhow) but by providing improved products and services. From this germ of an ideal all else has followed through an intricate maze of terminology, which currently is expressed by terms such as "competitive advantage" and "expert systems."

Computers and later computer/communications networks are the foundation of the "information age," which actually isn't such a bad term when compared with alternatives such as "space age," "electronic era," and "global village," to say nothing of "technetronic age" (coined by Zbigniew Brzezinski) and "superindustrial society" (used by Toffler). Fundamental to the employment of computer/communications technology is the fact that the cost of computers is declining as the cost of human labor is rising. The implication of this is that the primary objective of the technology—both in the factory and in the office—is "saving money." The vision of the information age presented by the prophets not only has obscured this fact but, in this country, has unfortunately had the side effect of contributing to our becoming a debtor nation.

The volume of data being processed and the volume of information being transferred have led to the mistaken assumption that we are in the vanguard of the information age and that somehow it is all right if our industrial society deteriorates before our very eyes. The value of our industrial base is somehow confused with information about quarterly earnings projections, which are disseminated by brokers and analysts who are unfamiliar with either products or markets. The ability of computers to process enormous volumes of stock transactions becomes confused with practical knowledge of when to buy and sell. "Those who believe that observation of physical reality or consultation of data 'tells' us anything have misunderstood the basic lessons of methodology" (to quote Machlup once again). We had better understand these basic lessons before listening to either our machines or the information age prophets.

Let's take a few snapshots of what some of the prophets have had to say:

- Toffler in *The Third Wave* (Morrow, 1980) has a section on "Enhancing the Brain" which includes the following adjacent paragraphs. The first postulates that in an "intelligent environment" where "machines, appliances, and even walls are programmed to speak," it will be possible to employ the functionally illiterate as airline reservation clerks, stockroom personnel, machine operators, and repairpeople. The next states that computers will "enhance our mind-power as Second Wave technology enhanced our muscle-power." Later (after expressing fascination because he is writing his book on a word processor), he looks forward to the day when an advertisement for a "Group Vice President" will state that typing is required.

- John Naisbitt has become a prophet of the coming information age by counting the number of times various technological "trends" are mentioned in selected newspapers—a sort of technological best-seller list that is completely unrelated to what is said about these trends. Get enough mentions in the press and you have a megatrend on your hands. People pay for this "information," and except for one lonely Harper's author (Emily Yoffe, *Harper's*, September 1983), no one seems to have bothered to question the methodology. You can't create reality by writing about it or prophesying it, much less by observing what is being written or said about it.

5.3 THE PRAGMATISTS

IBM may have started us on the road to this "information age" craze, but IBM has a substantial customer base that demands more practical results. Pragmatism is the product of experience, and those who have had the following experiences usually view the "information age" with less than unbounded enthusiasm.

- Executives who find that even "bread and butter" computer applications fail; for example, the president of US Sprint, who reportedly lost his job in 1987 because the company lost control of accounts receivable.

- Everyone familiar with the problems of productivity in the systems development process and the "solutions" to those problems; for example, the consulting firm, client, software vendor, and users of the New Jersey 4GL automobile registration system, which was so slow that an ever-increasing backlog of transactions developed, and which was of such poor quality that the integrity of the data base was destroyed.

- Systems personnel, who are gradually finding out what ease-of-use is all about. For example, two major universities installed "advanced" telephone systems, only to find that they became a major source of dissatisfaction because nobody could figure out how to use them. (As one information systems executive quizzically observed: "Have you ever been confronted with announcing a training program for college professors on how to use the telephone?")

- Managerial and professional users of personal computers who become dependent on them in their work; for example, those who become exposed to the complexity and effort required to (1) distribute data to those with incompatible hardware-software systems and (2) maintain their personal data bases.

- Those who use computers (and information) for competitive advantage and find that the "system" can get out of control; for example, the stock market during 1987—a lesson some of those involved may or may not have learned.

The list could go on and on, but any intelligent person who has been involved in situations similar to this, even if only as an observer, inevitably becomes a pragmatist or a cynic, or begins to giggle uncontrollably at the oddest moments. IBM has more information on the limits of computer/communications technology than any other organization in the world. I believe that SAA is the pragmatic expression of what must be done to establish the infrastructure necessary to control data entropy; supporting the "information age" prophesies of the visionaries will require even more.

5.4   MULTIPLE MESSIAHS

Regardless of whether you listen to the prophets or the pragmatists of the information age, the vendors are the messiahs who must deliver the promises. The directions of the major messiahs are shown in Figure 5.2. Their messages can be summarized as follows:

- Apple is saying "create," Digital Equipment (DEC) is saying "communicate," and IBM is saying "cooperate." Fundamentally, these messages come from their hardware orientations.

  - The graphics capability of the personal computer becomes the focus for a multimedia view of the world. The emphasis becomes form rather than substance. That is what Apple, desktop publishing, and HyperCard are all about. Despite talk about "intelligent documents," creativity implies doing your own thing, thinking little about the inevitable high entropy of the output (whether on a screen or a piece of paper).

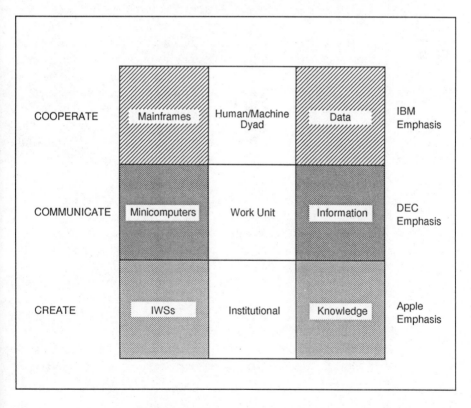

Figure 5.2 – Where They Are Leading Us

Source: Killen & Associates, Inc.

- The communications capability of the minicomputer and its associated software has led DEC to advise: "build the network first and hang the computers on later." This is really like saying you should start communicating before you have any idea what you are going to say—or to whom. (Somewhat like moving your mouth before your mind is engaged.) The ability to move, direct, and/or distribute vast amounts of data and/or information (by my definitions) does not imply quality at all. Communications for communications' sake is what information overload, junk mail, telephone solicitation, and pornographic phone messages are all about.

- The sharing of large mainframes has established a tradition of managed cooperation among the users of shared resources— processing power, data, communications facilities, output devices, etc. IBM is fully aware that no resource or user is an island, whether on a single mainframe or on an international network, and that some form of managed cooperation must be enforced. It takes energy to maintain order in a high-entropy environment, and the distributed data base environment has high entropy. Most people, including those in IBM, would prefer to ignore this fact, but that doesn't make it any less true.

• Some time ago, DEC and Apple announced that they would cooperate to make VAXs talk with Macintoshes. Fine and good. But considering the primary orientation of each of them, it is doubtful that either organization understands or can solve the problems of distributed data resources. Both have concentrated on generation and distribution of information, with minimal regard for data quality. Fortunately, most of their systems have been installed in environments where complex data management has not been required. With increased emphasis on integrated systems, electronic data interchange, and hierarchical networks, the environments that consider unmanaged data acceptable are shrinking rapidly.

• John Sculley was once quoted as saying that SAA was "too little and too late." This could be either a case of ignorance as to what SAA is, or a simple case of whistling as one approaches the cemetery. It is probably a little bit of both. However, regardless of the packaging and advertising, you don't sell many cans of a liquid plumbing product for soda pop. Either IBM is spending billions of dollars to solve problems that do not (and never will) exist or there will be some unpleasant surprises for those unwary customers who attempt to implement integrated corporate systems using the "create" and "communicate" strategies of Apple and DEC—either combined or separately.

Perhaps I should add a fourth "messiah" to this situation—Sun Microsystems. The Sun message would naturally be "calculate." However, that message is as old as computers, and this book is about data. Practically every computer architect has started with the assumption that if you can just compute fast enough, you will solve all the world's problems. In the commercial data processing world, every user has learned about "garbage in, garbage out." In 1989, Sun suffered some serious setbacks, which were attributed to "systems problems" (like accounting, forecasting, and order processing). I assume these problems were not because there were not enough MIPS to go around.

To summarize, IBM is in the unique position of being able to develop a solution and then create (or at least define) a problem. If my analysis of the ultimate objectives of SAA and IBM's distributed data base strategy are correct, this will be a classic illustration of this capability. You will be surprised how rapidly data base integrity and security will become major problems in the marketplace as soon as IBM has its own house in order. The next chapter is not recommended for fainthearted competitors or customers of IBM.

6

IBM's Single-Site Data Base Strategy

IBM's overall plan for transparent interconnected data bases comprises two sets of strategies.

The first set of strategies provides data base management system products to three systems categories—mainframes, minicomputers, and intelligent workstations—for single-site data base or stand-alone data base requirements. I call this IBM's single-site data base strategy.

The second set of strategies, which is basically an extension of the first, provides distributed functions to transparent interconnected data bases across networks of multiple sites. I call this IBM's distributed data base strategy.

IBM's dual strategy allows it to enhance its mainline data base management systems while it develops solutions that will meet the greater needs of the corporation.

This chapter presents IBM's single-site data base strategy, and Chapter 7 will present IBM's distributed data base strategy.

6.1 THE SINGLE-SITE DATA BASE STRATEGY FOR MAINFRAMES

While IBM's single-site data base strategy provides products for mainframes, minicomputers, and IWSs, revenues from the sale of single-site data base systems for mainframes that use the MVS operating system dwarf the same type of revenues for the minicomputer and IWS categories.

IBM has two data base strategies for the MVS environment: (1) To continue to support and enhance the hierarchical IMS data base product family and (2) to enhance the 5-year-old relational DB2 data base product family.

The objective of the MVS/IMS strategy is primarily to meet the' needs of existing customers. This customer base provides IBM with considerable income each year, and it is important that IBM keep them happy.

The objective of the MVS/DB2 strategy is primarily to obtain new customers, but also to support existing customers and to lay the foundation for the distributed data base environment.

The responsibility for developing and enhancing IMS and DB2 rests with IBM's Programming Systems line of business (LOB). The location for most of this work is IBM's Santa Teresa Labs in San Jose, CA.

IBM has another data base strategy to support the mainframes that use the VM operating system. Here, the objective is to obtain new customers for the smaller 370 products and to support the large base of SQL/DS customers under VM.

6.1.1 The MVS/IMS Hierarchical Data Base

The hierarchical data base product family consists of the data bases for the IMS Fast Path and the IMS Full Function and the Transaction Managers. After approximately 20 years of development, IMS is a robust data base management system that has high availability, high capacity, high performance (by IBM standards), and high use, with more than 10,000 systems installed throughout the world. As a group, these customers have invested billions of dollars in IMS data files, application programs, procedures, and people.

IBM continues to improve the capabilities of IMS. In 1987 it made several enhancements, most of which contributed to improving IMS's capacity and performance. For example, IBM announced that IMS Fast Path could process about a thousand transactions per second on a dedicated 3090-400. A typical IMS transaction is a point-of-sale application—authorization, credit-limit checks, and debit processing. IBM will continue to improve the capacity and performance of IMS and will improve IMS's usability, especially in a mixed IBM data base environment, i.e., an IMS/DB2 environment.

6.1.2 The MVS/DB2 Relational Data Base

IBM's relational product family under MVS consists of DB2, the SQL programming language, and the QMF query language. DB2 is optimized for the MVS/XA environment. It supports very large data bases and partitions; therefore, it is suited for future application requirements. Because of its relational features, many types of applications can be developed in a fraction of the time required to develop an IMS application. IBM plans to continue enhancing DB2 so that customers will develop more and more new applications using DB2 rather than IMS or competitors' products. This means that IBM will enhance security and authorization features as well as the backup and recovery capabilities expected of an industrial-strength data base manager, and it will continue to improve system performance. The company has also added features to ease some of the problems of working in an IMS and DB2 mixed environment.

Improvements in DB2's transaction processing performance will be incremental, and its performance will not surpass that of IMS. DB2's relational technology uses more machine cycles than the hierarchical data base management system, and IMS will continue to improve as well.

6.1.3 Positioning IMS and DB2 in the Market

Although IMS is an extremely important product, DB2 is IBM's strategic MVS data base. The relational technology of DB2 can meet the long-term data base management needs of customers, and it is essential for interconnecting or distributing data bases.

On the other hand, IBM must enhance IMS to protect the investments of its many customers (and ensure that IBM keeps its old business). A large number of them have a huge investment in IMS data files, applications programs, procedures, and people.

Both products, DB2 more than IMS, enable IBM to pursue new business. An enhanced IMS enables IBM to compete for applications that require very high availability (24-hour), high capacity, high performance, and low-cost per transaction. An enhanced DB2 can be used for almost all new applications. In the past, a customer would have used IMS or a competitor's data base management product for them. Enhancing DB2 also serves to strategically position IBM's customers for distributed data bases. It is usually impractical to develop and operate applications with distributed data bases unless they utilize relational technology.

6.1.4 Advantages and Disadvantages of a Dual Product Strategy

The dual MVS data base strategy has advantages and disadvantages. The advantage is that IBM is paid either way. The disadvantage is that IBM must support two major software systems, and many customers must do the same. This costs IBM and the users of those mixed MVS data bases a small fortune.

Offering two data bases causes some confusion in the marketplace. Many of IBM's customers don't know which data base to invest in. IBM's strategy is to encourage customers to consider DB2 first if they are installing new applications or if their existing applications are at the end of their life cycles and must be redesigned. IBM believes that DB2 will satisfy most customer applications. As IBM continues to enhance DB2, this will become increasingly true.

However, if DB2 is not suited for an application, and if availability is key (the application must function 24 hours a day, 7 days a week without fail), the choice is IMS. If capacity is key (a customer has voluminous data and needs quick response time and fast throughput), the choice is also IMS. If the customer's application package is built on IMS, then obviously the choice is IMS.

6.1.5 VM/SQL/DS

SQL/DS is the relational data base management system that runs under VM on the System/370. The responsibility for SQL/DS belongs to Programming Systems. Development activities are mostly located in Endicott, NY. All the usual issues, such as availability, capacity, performance, and other factors, pertain to this product.

6.2   THE SINGLE-SITE DATA BASE STRATEGY FOR MINICOMPUTERS

While the Programming Systems line of business concentrates on mainframe systems and the high end of the minicomputer category, the Application Business Systems Division provides data base product solutions for minicomputers—System/36, System/38, and the AS/400 products (Figure 6.1). The division concentrates on the OS/400.

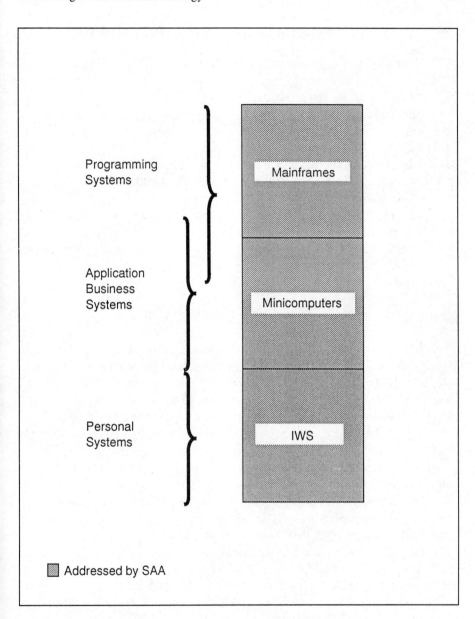

Figure 6.1 – Data Base Products by System

Source: Killen & Associates, Inc.

6.3   THE SINGLE-SITE DATA BASE STRATEGY FOR IWSs

IBM's Personal Systems Division (Entry Systems and the Advanced Workstation Division) supports data base product solutions for both the PS/2 and AIX workstation products.

Personal Systems is responsible for developing the Data Manager, a relational data base management system that was initially bundled with the OS/2 EE. (As I write this chapter, executives at IBM are speculating about whether they should unbundle the Data Manager from the OS/2 EE operating system. This is clearly a sign that the bundled version has not been selling well.)

Personal Systems will eventually support as many as three DBMSs for AIX—one each for small, medium, and large requirements. IBM's Programming Systems LOB (and STL) is helping to ensure that the interfaces to the AIX DBMSs are consistent with the interfaces to the SAA data bases—DB2, SQL/DS, and the Data Manager.

6.4   CONSISTENT IMPLEMENTATION

IBM's objective is to offer customers consistent implementations of SQL, QMF, and other important data base related software across the company's relational data bases—DB2, DS, the Data Manager (PC), and the Data Manager (AIX). Figure 6.2 shows the four SAA strategic environments, the relational data bases, and the SQL programming interface.

This consistency of implementation is extremely important because it allows application software to be (more) easily migrated from one relational data base environment to another, with consistent results. However, obtaining consistency is easier said than done.

It is difficult for programmers to implement software consistently, even if they work on the same project in the same building. Groups use different life cycles and tools. One person doesn't want to use another's code, etc. IBM faces all these problems, and more. Developing a consistent implementation of SQL and QMF across the different product families is no small project. To complicate things, programming groups may be located in ten different facilities, including Santa Teresa; Toronto, Canada; Austin, TX; and Rochester, MN.

Programming Systems' Santa Teresa Labs developed DB2 and is now helping AIX developers to implement consistent SQL and QMF across AIX data base management systems.

6.5 ARCHITECTURES

Architectures play a major role in IBM's strategies to develop data base management products. If we understand the architectures that IBM uses in developing its data products strategy, we know the framework for IBM's strategy.

The architectures used as the bases for IBM's data base product strategies are SAA, Software Structure, and Data Base Management Architecture. I will briefly comment on each of these and their importance.

6.5.1 Systems Application Architecture

Since 1987, IBM has mandated that all its relational data base and mainline programming products conform to SAA. Through SAA, IBM is

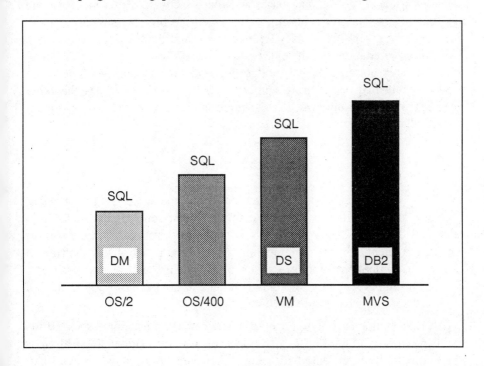

Figure 6.2 – The Four SAA Data Base Environments

Source: Killen & Associates, Inc.

attempting to create a common programming interface and a common communications interface for each of the relational data bases. The CPI specifies the data base, dialog, presentation, and query interfaces that SAA will support for relational data bases. A common communications interface simplifies the task of writing programs that address the DBMSs across SAA. All these standards are needed to simplify the task of developing applications in a multiproduct environment. All of them are also needed to simplify the task of developing distributed data base applications.

6.5.2 Software Structure

Three of IBM's lines of business use IBM's Software Structure in developing the relational data bases and other software. Software Structure has four layers: operating systems (also called the blue layer), communications (yellow layer), data bases (green layer), and applications (red layer). This structure enables the developer of a 370 MVS transaction manager to think not only about how that product interfaces with other MVS software products, but also about how it interfaces with products across the other three software environments. It is an important tool that IBM uses to manage software development.

6.5.3 Data Base Management Architecture

The same three lines of business also use the same Data Base Management Architecture to manage the software components that make up a relational data base. By components I mean optimizer, data base management component, data communication system, data dictionary, distributed data base component, and other constituents. This architecture drives a consistent implementation of relational data base technology to each of the four operating environments (Figure 6.3).

This feature is important now, but when IBM accelerates its efforts to interconnect the data bases, it will be even more critical. If IBM finds chaos upon lifting the hood of each of the data bases, it will have difficulty making changes. The Data Base Management Architecture provides the structure needed to manage the development of all four IBM relational data bases effectively.

6.6   SUMMARY

IBM has a single-site data product strategy for each of the three systems categories: mainframes, minicomputers, and IWSs. For the mainframe category, IBM executes two MVS single-site data base product strategies—one for the hierarchical IMS data base and another for the relational DB2 data base—and a strategy for supporting SQL/DS under VM. For the minicomputer, IBM has a relational data strategy for OS/400. For the IWS category, IBM offers the Data Manager under OS/2 and several Data Managers under AIX.

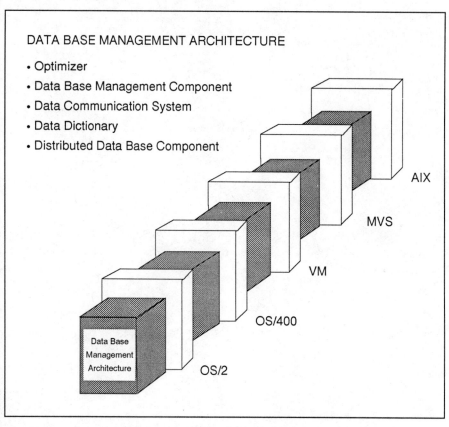

Figure 6.3 – Data Base Management Architecture

Source: Killen & Associates, Inc.

7

IBM's Distributed Data Base Strategy

As mentioned previously, IBM's distributed data base strategy is an extension of its single-site data base strategy. The DDB strategy offers everything that customers want in single-site data bases, i.e., availability, performance, security, recovery, data definition, integrity, transparency, and optimization, and expands them across an entire network of data bases.

This chapter discusses the background of IBM's distributed data base technology, a framework for understanding the different classifications of distributed data base technology, and customer requirements.

7.1 FOUNDATION AND BACKGROUND OF DDBs

In the late 1960s, IBM developed a prototype relational data base called System R, which turned out to be one of IBM's most ambitious technical undertakings. Probably no computer company but IBM would have had the resources to undertake a project of this magnitude. However, the scope of System R was limited to a single-site relational data base.

IBM's next technological step was to advance the stand-alone System R, not only into commercial relational products but into distributed environments through a research project—R*. The goal of R* was to build a distributed data base system of cooperating but autonomous sites, each of which would support a relational data base system. R* research efforts provided IBM, as well as other developers of "distributed" data base products, with many of the concepts and principles that underlie the development and operations of commercial "distributed" data base products.

The most important object of R* was site autonomy. This autonomy is achieved when (1) each site is able to control accesses from other sites to its own data and to manipulate its data without being conditioned by any other site, and (2) the system is able to grow incrementally and to operate continuously with new sites joining existing ones, without agreement between them on global data structures or definitions.

The R* research project produced the technology to enable each site to control access to its own data. However, the ability of each site to manipulate its data without being conditioned by any other site has only partially been achieved. This is because the loss of site autonomy cannot be avoided during the two-phase commitment of transactions. A key tenet of IBM's distributed data products is that the network must operate continuously as changes are made.

7.1.1 What Was Learned from R*?

The implementations of a version of R* by IBM and some of its customers promoted understanding of the requirements of a distributed data base environment and development of the concepts and principles that underlie the operation of distributed data bases. IBM learned, for example, that many distributed data base applications need to have the data base located at the site of the *last transaction* to minimize communications costs, based on the premise that additional transactions will be generated there. IBM also began to appreciate the need for referential integrity and for governors to control the remote demands for resources made upon a local site.

The R* research and trial installations also made IBM aware that a distributed data base environment is very demanding and that a quick implementation of some or all of R*'s features would only result in a "research"-grade distributed data base—one unsuited to running a company's business.

Fundamental to the success of IBM's DDB strategy is convincing potential customers that they need an "industrial-strength" distributed data base and that a "research"-grade distributed data base has shortcomings. I leave it to IBM and its competitors to argue their own case.

7.2   IBM'S DDB DIRECTION—CLASSES OF PRODUCTS

The scope of IBM's distributed data base strategy encompasses four IBM SAA operating environments across the mainframe, minicomputer, and intelligent workstation product categories. The products in the mainframe category are MVS, VM, and, depending on price, the OS/400 product family. The minicomputer category consists of the OS/400 and, depending on price, some low-end 370 products. The IWS category consists of the OS/2.

Some people might point out that the increasingly popular AIX RISC System/6000 family should be included in the IWS and/or minicomputer categories. I omitted the RS/6000 deliberately. In the Preface of this book I defined a distributed data base environment. I repeat that definition here: "Such systems, I believe, will be based on systems that manage distributed data bases. I define a system that effectively supports a distributed data base environment as one that (1) allows for access and update of data across multiple computer systems platforms, (2) enables users to access and update data on multiple systems with a single transaction, without knowing where the data exist or the type of system on which they exist, and (3) provides the security and performance needed for this level of computing."

The last part of this definition, the part that deals with security, is why I omitted the UNIX-based RS/6000. The nature of UNIX works against security. A key objective of UNIX development has been to develop and use standard interfaces and software. IBM has repeatedly stated that it will support standard products developed by the Open Software Foundation (OSF), but I doubt that it will ever actively support any OSF product that is developed specifically for security purposes. The use of "standard" software works against security because too many programmers know too much about the software.

The nature of the UNIX computing community also works against security. Much of the traditional UNIX computing community has always believed in a highly accessible and open computing environment. They believe in ease of access to not only their own networks but other networked resources as well. Many want the UNIX environment to remain that way. However, while ease of access makes it possible to quickly access resources, it also makes it possible for a hacker in Tokyo to penetrate UNIX networks throughout the United States—even military networks.

Many vendors and support groups (including IBM, UNIX International, and the OSF) are working to improve the security of UNIX systems. However, in my opinion, not even all their efforts can make the RS/6000 secure in the foreseeable future—at least not secure enough for distributed data bases.

I believe that IBM understands the UNIX security issue, and I think this is the main reason IBM does not include AIX-based computers in its distributed data base environment. Other reasons include the fact that IBM has a large base of existing customers under MVS, VM, OS/400, and OS/2 that need distributed functionality. Very few RS/6000 customers need it at this time.

With respect to SAA distributed data bases, customers should view the AIX RS/6000 as a node on the periphery of the SAA network. To help maintain the security of commercial systems, customers should limit the transfer of data on the RS/6000 to file transfers.

IBM is working to add distributed functionality to each family of SAA platforms so that products within a homogeneous family can work together (Figure 7.1). For example, it is adding distributed data base functionality to permit MVS–MVS, VM–VM, OS/400–OS/400, and OS/2–OS/2

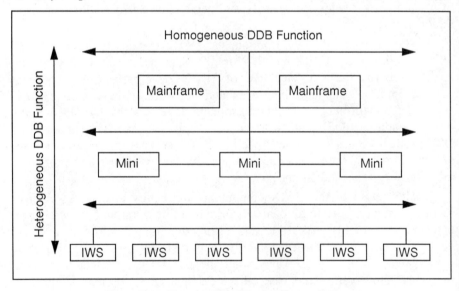

Figure 7.1 – Homogeneous/Heterogeneous Systems

Source: Killen & Associates, Inc.

homogeneous environments. IBM's announcement of the Remote Relational Access Facility will enable as many as eight SQL/DS data bases on VM systems to provide some distributed data base function.

IBM is providing distributed functionality to each of the SAA families of products to enable customers to build distributed data base systems that consist of disparate products. Each year, IBM announces products that provide additional functionality for heterogeneous environments.

7.3   IBM'S DDB DIRECTION—LEVELS OF DDB FUNCTIONS

No customer wants to distribute data bases just for the sake of distributing data. Instead, customers consider distributing data bases or acquiring distributed data base functionality to obtain new capabilities that produce greater productivity, improve decision making, lower costs, and provide other benefits. IBM's DDB strategy aims to provide increased distributed data base function.

Figure 7.2 categorizes the various levels of distributed data base function and the difficulty of developing that functionality. Although I do

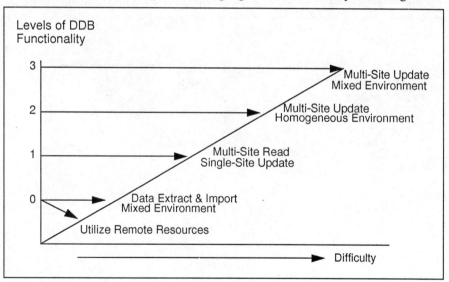

Figure 7.2 – Distributed Function

Source: Killen & Associates, Inc.

not purport to present a definitive classification of the various levels of distributed data base function, this description will give the reader some basis for thinking about the various flavors of distributed data base functions and an appreciation for the difficulty encountered in developing this functionality.

7.3.1 Level 0: Utilize Remote Resources, Extract and Import Remote Data

At this level, a customer (1) shares resources or distributes some function to multiple sites, and (2) can extract data from a remote site and import them to a local site. Many people would consider this to be less than a distributed data base function. The utilization of resources is shown in Figure 7.3.

7.3.1.1 Level 0: Utilize Remote Resources

When customers want to utilize remote resources, they must distribute the data function to another site. Consider a customer that has built an

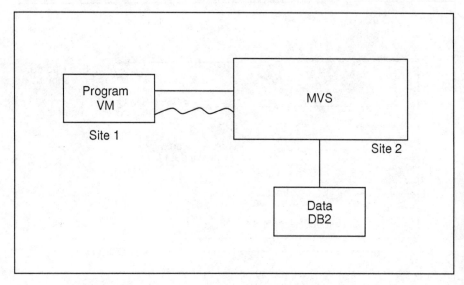

Figure 7.3 – Utilization of Resources

Source: Killen & Associates, Inc.

application on a VM machine. Later, he finds that the number of users on the system has increased and that the data base has become a critical component. The customer wants to keep the program on the VM system but wants to move the data to a more robust environment—a DB2–MVS environment. This is a more efficient use of his resources.

7.3.1.2 Level 0: Extract and Import Remote Data

Often data must be obtained from a remote site and used at a local site. A common example is when a customer has data in DB2 on an MVS system and can access either locally attached personal computers or a local area network (LAN) of personal computers via a server workstation. The personal computer users may simply want to extract data from the DB2 and import them into a spreadsheet like Lotus 1-2-3 or into a full-blown applications program. The LAN configuration is presented in Figure 7.4.

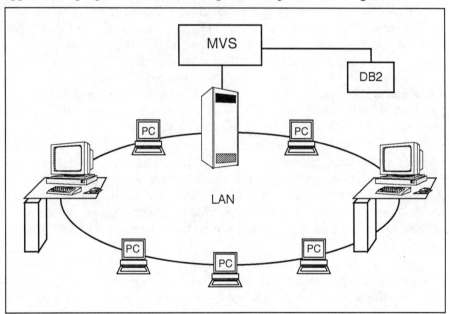

Figure 7.4 – LAN Configuration

Source: Killen & Associates, Inc.

7.3.2 Level 1: Multi-Site Read, Single-Site Update, Homogeneous Environment

Another common need of customers is to read from more than one site and to update a single site. A customer may have ten DB2 sites and want to read sales data from nine sites into the tenth site. At the tenth site, a program produces a report. Presently, each site time-stamps the data and transmits or physically transports its tapes to the tenth site. This entire process can be automated to distributed data base functionality by enabling the tenth system to execute a multi-site read and single-site update.

This function is relatively easy to provide in a homogeneous environment.

7.3.3 Level 2: Multi-Site Update, Homogeneous Environment

Certain businesses need the capability of updating multiple sites. Consider the problem facing a bank when a customer instructs it to withdraw funds from an account in New York and deposit them in an account in California. Both data bases need updating. This is a significant challenge because between the time the New York office makes its withdrawal update and the California office makes its deposit update, anything could happen: AT&T's lines might go down, IBM's computer system at either end might malfunction, an earthquake might shake up California, or some other devastating event might occur. Needless to say, the system must have the capability to recover from such disasters.

To perform multi-site updates, the system must first determine whether all systems can commit to the update. There may be 10,000 personal computers on a network, each scheduled for an update. If something goes wrong, the system must be able to back out of all updates. In other words, the system must be able to provide a two-phase commitment with system integrity. Making a system like this work requires the use of midrange systems.

Today, IBM can perform a two-phase commitment on data bases on a single central processing unit (CPU), and it is expanding that function across multiple sites to provide multi-site update with system-provided integrity. (Chapter 10 will review IBM's DDB progress and capability.)

To provide and use multi-site update, vendors and users will have to come to grips with new issues relating to authorization, security, resource allocation, and other factors. Before customers start using a multi-site updating function, they must answer difficult questions about distributed data base environments, such as: How do I control this? How do I know that the user updating my data base in Site 2 is authorized? Who gave the authorization?

An entirely different set of problems exists for handling multi-site updates.

7.3.4 Level 3: Multi-Site Update, Mixed Environment

In the near future, customers will increasingly need to execute multi-site updates in a mixed environment. This will require some additional distributed data base functionality and will be more difficult to achieve than a multiple update of a homogeneous environment will be.

7.4 SUMMARY

The R* research project provided a foundation of technology with which IBM could develop distributed data base products. The products available from IBM today enable customers to implement only the lowest levels of distributed data functionality. IBM is enhancing the distributed data function for homogeneous environments, and in the future will do so for mixed heterogeneous environments. When companies begin to develop products for multi-site update, they must already have found answers to the problems of accountability, security, and other basic data base issues that will be exacerbated by the coming of distributed data base functions.

8

Analysis of IBM's Distributed Data Base Strategy

8.1   IBM'S PERSPECTIVE

To understand IBM's strategy, we must look at things from IBM's point of view. From Figure 8.1, a diagram used earlier, we can make certain assumptions about IBM's current view of account control, which is closely related to how IBM will implement its DDB strategy.

- The main elements of IBM account control are associated with having established reasonably firm control over the corporate data bases that are used for corporate planning and, therefore, for institutional performance. This control has been established and maintained by:
  - IBM's dominant position in the mainframe market
  - IBM's mainframe operating systems—both MVS/XA and VM
  - IBM's mainframe data base management systems—both IMS and DB2
- Although the extent of IBM's control is not so obvious at the work unit level, IBM exercises partial control over "data base management" here by offering a full range of office products and multiple departmental processors. A work unit can be a small business as well as a "department" within a large organization. With this in mind, it is possible to identify a much maligned but significant asset that IBM has at this level.
  - The System/36 has an extensive and loyal customer base of several hundred thousand installed systems. These systems

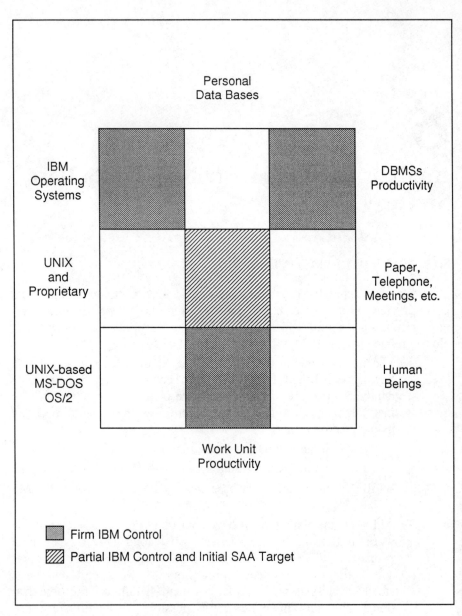

Figure 8.1 – IBM Account Control

Source: Killen & Associates, Inc.

are easy to use, have excellent networking capability, and, for purposes of "data base management," rely upon an "intuitive view" of data that is quite similar to and compatible with the relational model. (As explained previously, a deck of punch cards can be viewed as a table.) These systems are being used for practical business applications—accounting, payroll, inventory control, transaction processing of all kinds—as well as for the normal office productivity functions, such as word processing and electronic mail.

- The System/38 is substantially easier to use than the System/370, and its architecture includes addressing capability that goes well beyond that of MVS/XA. For data base management, "relational-like" capability has been built into the hardware. The System/38 was an outgrowth of IBM's abortive "future system" (FS) effort. Perhaps the future is now.

- It is important that IBM designated the System/3X as a major IBM computing environment when it announced SAA and that it designated "office systems" as the initial target of SAA. The System/3X is where business applications and office automation have already begun to be integrated. IBM knows this.

- Ken Olsen of Digital Equipment was once quoted as saying that the System/3X represents a "niche market." It is a "niche" that already has revenues larger than those of most of the computer manufacturers in the world, and in terms of distributed data bases, it represents the most important strategic square on my little chess board. Immediately following its announcement, the AS/400 generated approximately $5 billion worth of revenue for IBM in the last five months of 1988— some niche!

• While IBM is obviously sensitive to the twin threats of minicomputers and personal computers in terms of losing control of operating systems (see Figure 8.1), it is also aware that no competitive hardware vendor has a comprehensive data base strategy. In addition, the tendency to split out DBMSs as products, rather than tightly integrating them with operating systems (and hardware), has made it extremely difficult for minicomputer or personal computer vendors to implement an integrated strategy.

This is precisely the vulnerability that IBM will attempt to exploit with its distributed data base strategy.

• There are two areas over which neither IBM nor any other computer vendor currently exercises any significant control. Knowledge-based systems are in their infancy, and personal data bases are left up to the individual. Increasingly, we are combining personal data bases and corporate data bases (using PCs) to produce information (paper documents, messages, screens, etc.), which, in turn, we are combining with human knowledge to produce the decisions that affect institutional performance. The effect will not necessarily be positive for the following reasons:

– Current operating systems and DBMSs cannot control and manage the fragmented data that result from combining corporate and personal data bases using PCs. I use the term *fragmented data* because that is precisely what happens when various spreadsheet and data base management packages are used to process and store personal data bases; data can become fragmented across spreadsheet and data base files on a single personal computer, and even more so across a network of the beasts. The indiscriminate distribution of data to the level of PCs at best increases data entropy dramatically and can cause immediate chaos.

– Even supposing that the data distributed to PCs are reasonably well managed and responsibly processed, the information developed is unmanageable. Conventional manual systems and procedures are incapable of handling the volume of information we produce and even encourage by the use of "office automation."

– Both personal data bases and information overload increase work (much of it clerical in nature) at the professional, managerial, and administrative levels. Most studies of office productivity (especially those from vendors) ignore this fact.

• Being aware of these facts, IBM has maintained a strong centralized focus to its distributed processing strategy. And, as I have stated on numerous occasions, the PC revolution makes SNA and IBM's highly centralized approach look wise when one considers the alternatives. Through its operating systems and DBMSs, IBM controls the mainframe market and corporate data bases. This has many advantages for IBM, some of which may be fortuitous.

- It provides for elements of account control at the highest levels, which means it fits nicely with IBM's objectives.
- It happens to be technically justifiable because, without solutions for the problems of distributed data bases (as described earlier in this book), data bases tend to become fragmented when data are transferred from central data bases to PCs.
- IBM and the central information system's function can make a strong case that once data are distributed from these central data bases (to minicomputers and/or PCs), they become unmanageable. More important, data from these sources will not be accepted back into the central data bases (update) without being strictly controlled by the central function. Access does not imply update.
- It has provided the network operating system model that will be implemented to progress toward distributed data bases. The concept of layered operating systems modeled after SNA views the entire network as a single, large host computer.

8.2   THE PROBLEMS OF MANAGING DATA

In his presentation on "Distributed Data in the 1990s," Dr. Allan L. Scherr defines an exceptionally rich variety of data that must be considered for distribution (Figure 8.2). In fact, it validates my definition of data taken from Fritz Machlup—data are anything stored in a computer. Obviously, IBM (or at least Dr. Scherr) takes a similar broad view of data. This has many ramifications:

- The problems of managing distributed data bases take on proportions that are substantially beyond those associated with encoded data alone.
- IBM's distributed data base strategy must include the integration of current information and knowledge with data bases. Among the hardware and software needed for this integration are:
  - Optical memories for storing the enormous volumes of data that are implicit in the broad definition of data
  - Increasingly intelligent peripherals for capturing and/or displaying these data

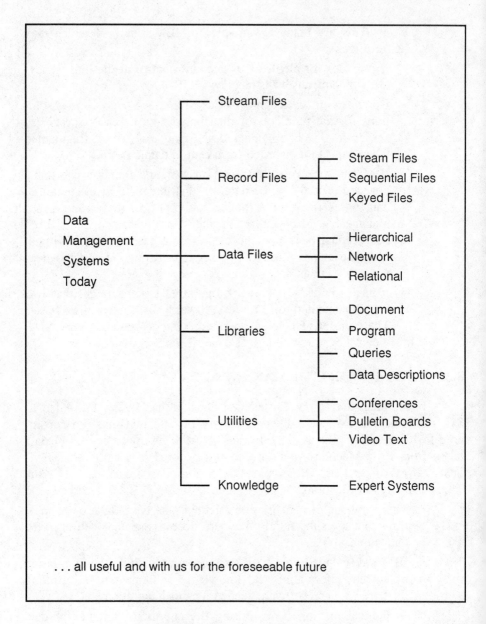

Figure 8.2 – Organizing and Accessing Data

Source: Killen & Associates, Inc.

- Increasingly intelligent programs to capture, screen, and disseminate the information and knowledge that currently exist and to manage the resulting vast reservoir of data.

Without belaboring the point, we can say that IBM is trying to solve an entirely different problem from the one its competitors are trying to solve. It is all fine and good for Ken Olsen of DEC to talk about "building the networks first and hanging the computers on later" and for John Sculley of Apple to state of SAA that "it is far too little, far too late," but one must question either their understanding of the problem or their sincerity. Creating and moving these new "data" are not the solution, they are a substantial part of the problem of distributed data manageability—which is to say that the integration of HyperCard and DECNet will not solve the problems of distributed data base management.

In *The Unwritten Comedy*, Phenella stated:

To be ignorant of many things is to be expected.

To know that you are ignorant of many things is the beginning of wisdom.

To know the category of things of which you are ignorant is the beginning of learning.

To know the details of that category of things of which you were ignorant is to no longer be ignorant.

The problems associated with distributed data bases have not necessarily been solved. However, at this point in time, IBM seems to be demonstrating substantially less ignorance of these problems than its competitors.

8.3   THE SOLUTION

In his presentation, Scherr looked at past and current IBM solutions to the problems of distributed data and, after noting their deficiencies, outlined tomorrow's solutions. He stated that yesterday's solutions were "pairwise" connections and could be categorized as follows:

- Application-to-application connections were developed by hand-tailoring (programming) the solution. This is what has been done with operational data bases in major transaction processing systems. It can be done, but it is expensive.
- Virtual disks where DASD (direct access storage device) is shared could serve as a rough connection between two systems,

but data are not really shared in such an environment. There are always trade-offs between disk space and performance of systems that literally share data. The result is redundant and unmanaged data.

- Simple file transfer between systems has been and continues to be used as a pairwise connection. I believe that bulk data movement is all that is required for some applications, and it will continue to be used in support of the distributed data environment. Scherr goes on to point out the deficiencies:

    - The efficiency of the solution is a function of the percentage of the data that is actually needed. (This problem will become even more apparent with electronic filing, where entire files will be requested for browsing in the same manner as paper files are now.)

    - There is no multinode concurrency (the data base synchronization problem and the obvious problems with micro-mainframe links and most minicomputer networks).

    - And, once again, the problem of redundant and unmanaged data is inherent in the "solution."

UNIX, having gained enormous public relations momentum in the last two years, is essentially confined to simple file transfer. Therefore, it is also subject to the deficiencies that Scherr points out. Progress beyond this point would require that not only UNIX but data base management systems as well, be standardized. In this regard, the prospect of progress among various hardware-software vendors remains dismal at best.

Scherr outlined today's solution as the "architected cross-system file models" as implemented in IBM's Distributed Data Management (DDM) product. This is a published architecture that permits S/36 and S/38 users to function as both requestors and servers for one another and to have access to System/370 systems operating under MVS/CICS as a DDM server. This current architecture has the following attributes:

- Record-at-a-time access across supported systems

- Local and remote transparency as to file location

- Concurrency maintained among both local and remote users

- A manageable single copy of data, even though they are distributed across the nodes

- A published architecture so that applications can be readily built to its specifications[1]

For tomorrow's solutions, Scherr proposes "architected cross-system data base models" with the following attributes:

- All the data types outlined in Figure 8.2
- Consistent SQL interfaces
- Consistent end-user interfaces
- Data administration facilities for:
  - Data description
  - Security
  - Recovery
  - Auditability
- Automatic data conversions across systems and applications
- Intersystem data integrity and recovery

Figure 8.3 presents the critical square among the major issues that SAA and distributed data base management begin to address. "Office systems" and business systems will meet at the office or work unit, as applications and data are distributed over the processor hierarchy. I believe that the System/3X will play the key role in this scenario.

All the supported IBM computing environments will be tightly integrated with "architected cross-system data base models" as defined by Scherr. This integration will occur at various levels within each system's hardware/firmware/software. These levels will include:

- The Application Manager level, which will handle scheduling, resource allocation, and commitment control across physical systems boundaries for various requestor–server combinations. (This assures that all necessary network resources—3090s, 9370s, PS/2s, and/or System/3Xs in any combination—are available to run the particular application.)
- The Application Program level, which will handle the actual processing of the user's application. (This implies transferring necessary data, programs, and control information among the various processors as required.)

---

1. The above attributes have led some analysts to confuse DDM with distributed data bases. IBM has been among those who have corrected this impression.

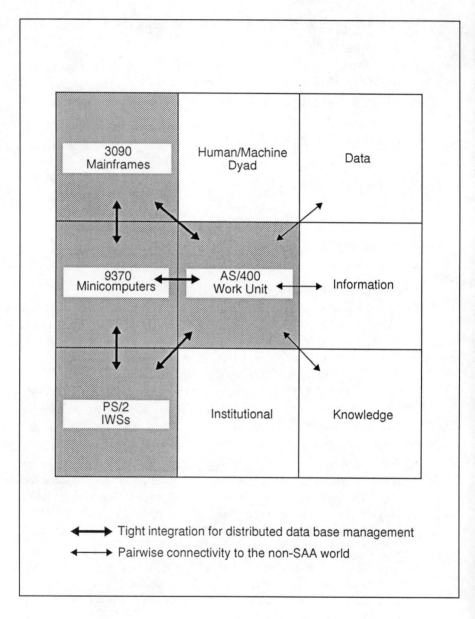

Figure 8.3 – The Critical Square

Source: Killen & Associates, Inc.

- The Request Manager level, which will assure location transparency, establish commitment control, and permit access planning across systems. (This is essential for what Chris Date states to be the fundamental principle of a distributed data base—"To the user, a distributed system should look exactly like a non-distributed system.")

- The Data Access Manager level, which will actually handle relational operations, data security, access optimization, and concurrency for the individual systems.

- The Data Storage Manager level, which will permit various processors (and applications) to share storage and which will optimize the use of storage access systems. (This implies the dynamic movement of data across the network to minimize server–requestor communications and is similar to the hierarchical storage management in virtual systems.)

- "Logical conversations" will be at the same level, with architected models at each level and architected messages and protocols between these levels.

The little black box at the center of the SAA architecture has been labeled *communications products* by IBM (Figure 2.1). The distributed data reference model described above rests on a "data connectivity facility" which will be at the heart of IBM's strategy. It ties SAA together by enabling distributed data base management. It brings together the IBM world as never before. It also presents unparalleled complications for software vendors. These will be presented later.

John Sculley criticized SAA by saying that it: "focuses defensively inward to connect everything IBM has, not outward to a multivendor market." To solve the problems inherent in distributed data base management as IBM perceives them, this is the only way to go, and even then it is an enormous technological undertaking. Connectivity (whatever it is taken to mean) does not address these problems, it merely provides yesterday's solution of "pairwise" connections to the outside world (Figure 8.3). It is difficult to say that IBM should be doing more when, actually, it is "betting the company" on SAA right now.

8.4   MY PERCEPTION OF IBM'S PERCEPTION

I think that IBM has an ambitious and technically sound approach to solving the problems of distributed data base management. However, much of my perception is based on the assumption that the System/3X will be the key to distributed data base management. That assumption is based on the following:

- The architecture of the System/38 is superior to that of the System/370 for a distributed data processing environment, and specifically for relational data base management systems.

- The System/36 and System/38 are already easier to network and use than are System/370 architecture systems.

- The architecture and ease of use of the System/3X will maintain and improve on the advantages listed above. The System/3X will be positioned as IBM's distributed data base engine and as its primary gateway to the outside world for pairwise connectivity (file transfer). This is essentially to say that the System/3X will be IBM's primary office system for the integration of data, information, and knowledge.

The proper distribution of processing and data over computer/communications networks is dictated by complex trade-offs associated with the following:

- Relative price–performance of the processors and their operating systems

- The structure and costs associated with the communications networks being used

- The ratio of data needed to data transferred

- Frequency and/or probability of access (use)

- The performance of the network in terms of its ability to provide adequate response time for the application

While there are also other factors that influence how data should be distributed over computer/communications networks, it is not necessary to go any farther to conclude that the success of any distributed data base strategy depends on the performance of an exceptionally complex set of hardware-software parameters. Experience tells us that our ability to predict the performance of complex systems has not been good, and unpleasant surprises on much simpler systems are the rule rather than the exception. Queueing network theory has proved itself a reasonably good predictor of operating systems performance (as Dr. Scherr discovered many years ago). However, presently, the world's experts on queueing theory are still developing the mathematics necessary to apply the theory to LANs. Distributed data bases, as they are evidently perceived by IBM, present a more complex problem.

Therefore, while SAA is a significant architectural and intellectual accomplishment, the question of whether or not it can be engineered remains. I believe that the advances and convergence of computer, communication, and storage technologies are achieving price–performance levels to support distributed data bases. The question now becomes software technology—that is what SAA is all about—and only IBM seems to have the necessary perception and resources to have a reasonable chance of making significant progress in the area.

Regardless of the degree to which IBM succeeds, one thing is clear—any symbiosis that existed with software-compatible hardware vendors or that is implied by the term "connectivity" will become a thing of the past. IBM is not going to provide a solution for distributed data base management for its competitors, and, indeed, it cannot. SAA signals that the free ride is over for everything but applications development in the strict sense of the word.

9

DDB from a Computer User's and Vendor's Perspective

When my company, Killen & Associates, Inc., published a report on SAA in October 1987, we sent a letter to end users which stated: "there is virtually no awareness among the user community of the importance of SAA. This is dangerous!" The letter went on to outline numerous "cases" that represented user reactions:

- The Einstein Case. SAA (like the Theory of Relativity) is so grand and all-encompassing that we do not understand it; therefore, it has no practical importance.

- The Hyperactive Child Case. SAA is just another case of vaporware. It really didn't say anything about delivery of the goodies to support the 386 chip. If I can't have it right now, it isn't worth anything.

- The Rorschach Test Case. SAA looks like SNA to me; therefore, I will be retired before it is important to my company.

- The Wall Street Analyst Case. I don't know why they are doing this SAA thing, whatever it is, but I do know that it is important enough for me to lower my IBM earnings projections for the next 20 quarters. (Fortunately, my spreadsheet package permits me to do this by clicking my mouse only twice, otherwise I might have to think about it.)[1]

---

1. The Wall Street Analyst Case was prepared before the dark days of October 1987. It is prophetic of the perils of the "information age."

• The Aging Technical Expert Case. SAA is just like everything else IBM has ever attempted to do with systems software—kludgey, big, slow, ill-conceived, unnecessary. I doubt that IBM will be able to do it, but if it does, it won't be any good.

The report then went on to say: "The list could go on and on. We could present The Macintosh Apple in Eden Case, The Relational Institutional Case, The Unqualified UNIX Enthusiast Case, The Unleash ISDN Now Case, The VAX to the MAX Case, The CASE Case, etc., and they would all have one thing in common—they would tend to denigrate SAA. Unfortunately, while they might be somewhat exaggerated cases, they would be surprisingly accurate representations of various user reactions to SAA."

User reactions to SAA have changed in the last two years. More has been revealed about SAA. Large users are beginning to say that they need SAA. The word is beginning to get out. SAA technical newsletters have been formed, and the founder of one was quoted as saying: "Every 10 to 12 years, IBM introduces a major new technology—one that is 'of major benefit' to the user and causes 'fear and loathing' on the part of its competitors. You can easily identify one of these unsettling introductions as the word 'architecture' is always involved." He went on to point out the examples of the 360 architecture and SNA.

An analysis of the SAA architecture has much in common with quantum mechanics. I stated when the report came out that if I was correct and the nucleus of SAA was distributed data bases, we could expect the initial reactions to distributed data bases to be similar to those to SAA. Users would initially fall into the classic "Einstein," "Hyperactive Child," and "Rorschach Test" cases. Financial analysts and "forecasters" would not understand the importance of what was going on, and competitors would be filled with "fear and loathing." All would be the same, except at a different level of complexity.

This observation has proved to be correct. One analyst has recommended that IBM "spin off" the AS/400 to concentrate on more promising business; another predicted that the replacement of the AS/400 with UNIX-based workstations is a "done deal"; a leading hardware vendor pronounced that distributed data bases "don't work"; and a leading DBMS vendor ran advertisements claiming that it has SAA "now," without so much as mentioning the AS/400.

(The March 15, 1991 issue of *Datamation* focused on 40 Years of Computing and failed to list the announcement of SAA as one of the industry's great events. I found this hard to understand.)

Initially, from the user's perspective, IBM's distributed data base strategy looks quite obscure, but users will soon recognize that it is "different" from other vendors' solutions. Then users will need to make major strategic decisions about whether or not distributed data bases have "major benefits" in their particular cases. And, as the computer/communications systems world becomes interconnected, these "benefits" should become clear. Perhaps the best way to place the user's view of IBM's DDB strategy in perspective is to project the complications that will be presented to competitive hardware and software vendors.

9.1   FROM A SOFTWARE VENDOR'S PERSPECTIVE

We cannot overestimate the complications of IBM's distributed data base strategy from the point of view of software vendors, but we can easily explain them. Fundamentally, the problems are those of the "logical conversations" at each level of the IBM "distributed data reference model," which was described in Chapter 8. A schematic of the data management reference model is presented in Figure 9.1. The tight vertical integration of data base management functions, operating systems, and applications functions are obvious in this diagram. In fact, the diagram could be more properly titled a "layered operating system."

As soon as the data management reference model is distributed, the problems become apparent to anyone familiar with systems programming and IBM operating systems (Figure 9.2). "Logical conversations" between requestor and server processes must occur at four levels in the model, and competitive operating systems and DBMSs will not be talking the same language. In fact, it would be fair to say that many competitive connectivity "solutions" will be deaf, dumb, and blind to what is going on in the IBM "data connectivity facility." Competitive, nonconforming software solutions can survive only at the applications level, and then only if they are developed in strict adherence to SAA standards.

The complications that IBM is presenting to software vendors go back to the fundamental concepts that shaped the computer itself. IBM's strategy uses software to present a common view of the IBM network as an integrated computer system with everything else connected as "peripherals." Consider the following:

- The fundamental concept of the von Neumann architecture is to bring programs and data together in common storage. In IBM's distributed data base environment, the "programmer" (software vendor) can assume that all his programs and data are already in common storage on the network. Any competitive systems will be viewed as peripherals, just as card readers, tape drives, and disk storage have traditionally been, and both programs and data must be imported to and exported from the central black box of the SAA architecture. These "I/O activities" are the most complex part of programming, just as they were in early computer

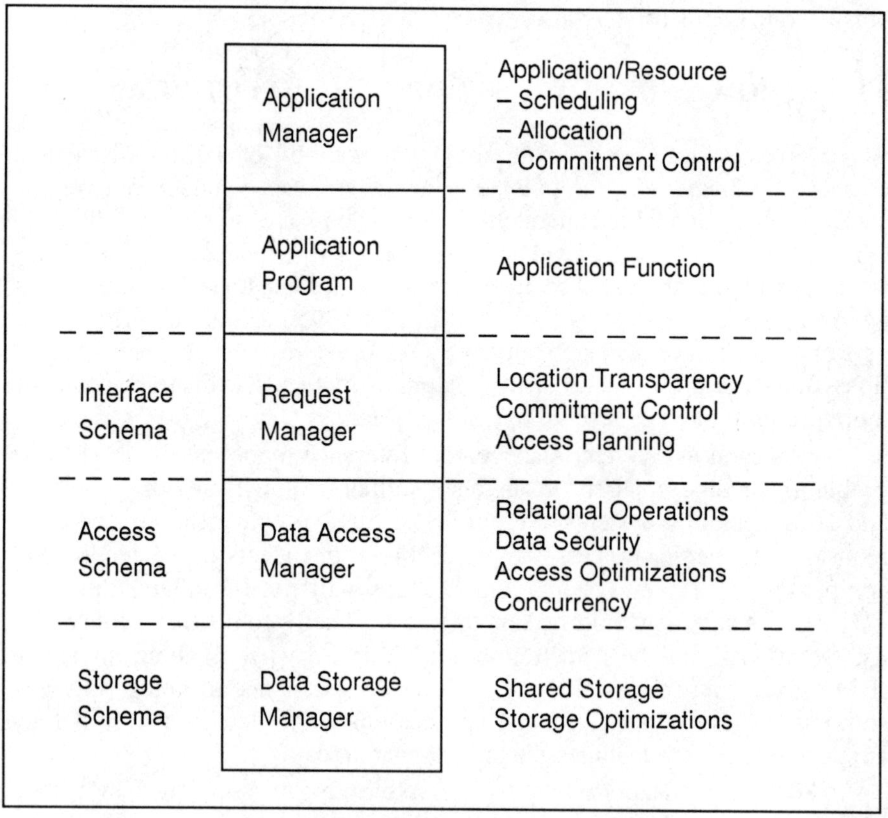

	Application Manager	Application/Resource – Scheduling – Allocation – Commitment Control
	Application Program	Application Function
Interface Schema	Request Manager	Location Transparency Commitment Control Access Planning
Access Schema	Data Access Manager	Relational Operations Data Security Access Optimizations Concurrency
Storage Schema	Data Storage Manager	Shared Storage Storage Optimizations

Figure 9.1 – A Data Management Reference Model

Source: Killen & Associates, Inc.

programming—that is the reason we have operating systems to begin with. So, either you take IBM's network operating system or you are confronted with building one yourself at an entirely different level.

- The fundamental concept of Norbert Wiener's cybernetics was the feedback loop. The biggest challenge of distributed data bases is to keep updates (feedback) in synchronization. IBM's distributed data base strategy promises to do that within its architecture. However, it cannot permit update from uncontrolled sources, nor can it accept responsibility for the updating of data

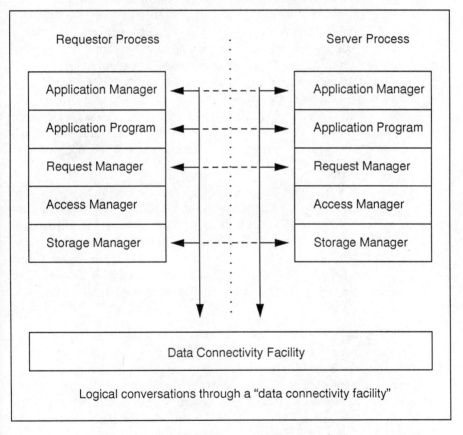

Figure 9.2 – A Distributed Data Reference Model

Source: Killen & Associates, Inc.

bases on competitive systems. Once again, accept IBM's network operating system and you can have feedback—otherwise,
program it yourself.

• The fundamental concept of Claude Shannon's information theory was entropy of information (signals) being communicated
over various communications media. (Von Neumann told him to
use the term "entropy" because no one would understand it any-
way, and that remains true to this day.) Fundamentally, the theory confirms the fact that the more ways things can be arranged,
the more energy is required to maintain order in the face of the
natural tendency toward chaos. In the current case, we are talking about communication between an IBM network that looks
like one big computer and any competitive systems that happen
to be "hung on." The potential for noise between the architected
protocols and messages that flow over IBM's "data connectivity
facility" and those that will flow over competitors' facilities will
be enormous. Entropy (the tendency toward chaos) increases
enormously outside of the SAA black box, and substantial
energy, both human and computer power, will be necessary to
prevent chaos.

• It all comes down to the simple fact that either you accept
IBM's strategy or you are confronted with a lot of work in connecting with IBM's network operating system for distributed
data base management. This is compounded enormously by the
fact that IBM doesn't have any incentive to make it easier. Competitive software vendors will be confronted with a constantly
shifting black box of hardware, firmware, software, and vaporware.

SAA is IBM's invitation to applications software vendors and customers to get dressed up and go to a dance at the country club. There will
be plenty of well-behaved operating system and DBMS debutantes ready
to trip the light fantastic with those who are willing to dance to the
"orchestrated (architected) models and schemas" at the Distributed Data
Base Management Ball as long as those invited observe the orderly protocols of the occasion. And, remember—Daddy has a lot of money.

What can those roughneck operating systems and DBMS vendors
who were not invited do? They have a number of alternatives:

- They can crash the party and pay the extremely high price of trying to buy their way into a society that goes back through innumerable generations of systems and DBMS software—only to find that they can never really keep up with the "Blue Book" set of MVS/XA (and the "XB"), VM, OS/2 Extended Edition, DB2, and all those surprises still hidden under the greater SAA umbrella.

- They can remain as uninvited guests and wait patiently on the sidelines for the distributed data reference model to crash on the dance floor like a bag of marbles and completely disrupt the whole shindig. After which, they can calmly proceed to pick up the fallen bodies.

- They can decide that the parking lot is a fine place to hold a dance and turn up their car radios full blast to detract from whatever is going on in the ballroom. In fact, several couples are already beginning to kick up a little gravel as DBMSs start to seek out new operating systems environments. And that maverick Gates kid is already out there with his stretch limousine full of rock stars just waiting to drown out the whole country club set.

To carry the analogy further, the UNIX party in the parking lot is attracting a lot of attention, and even the country club set is becoming distracted on their way to the DDBM Ball. However, some of the crowd is getting a little rowdy, and security isn't too good. Juvenile delinquents are beginning to wander freely among the crowd, sampling the wares of the various "users" and occasionally bringing the whole party to a halt with their mindless "games." Authorities have begun to make arrests, and some party sponsors are beginning to wonder how the more serious community members will react to all the noise being generated.

The fact remains that even the largest software vendors do not have either the technical or the financial resources to compete with IBM's distributed data base strategy. They can hope it fails either because of its implementation or because there is no need or market for it. For those who think they can implement SQL and their version of a relational database and sell these in the IBM distributed processing environment, there will be nothing but lasting frustration and red ink. IBM is telling the software vendors that there are big bucks to be made in developing applications that conform to SAA standards, but that there will be big problems

for competitive data base management systems at all levels of the processing hierarchy. Software vendors who don't understand this probably won't
survive anyhow.

9.2   FROM A HARDWARE VENDOR'S PERSPECTIVE

Hardware vendors will be confronted with the same technical perspectives as the software vendors, except that they are definitely unwanted
guests. In fact, it could be truthfully stated that the entire purpose of the
distributed data base strategy is to exclude them from the Distributed Data
Base Management Ball. The lure of the masked queen of the ball (connectivity) may attract some hardware vendors who feel they can coexist com-
fortably by tying in with the IBM computing environments, but they run a
substantial risk of becoming entangled in a complex and carefully architected web of "logical conversations," with some predictable consequences. The masked queen will turn out to have all the characteristics of
a black widow spider ready to dispose of both foreign species and former
mates.

A quick review of the major IBM computing environments reveals
some of the potential problems for hardware vendors.

- At the mainframe level, the software-compatible mainframe vendors who have helped make IBM mainframe software a standard
  will find it more difficult to maintain compatibility. For example,
  not too long ago IBM announced the Enterprise Systems Archi-
  tecture/370 (ESA/370), which is designed to provide the addressing capability necessary for the management of distributed data
  bases. The increase from 31- to 44-bit addressing increases
  addressable virtual storage from 2 billion bytes to over 16 tril-
  lion bytes. Competitive hardware and software vendors will need
  time to respond to this change.

- At the System/3X level, the System/38 already has 48-bit
  addressing and built-in relational capability, which are more
  attractive in a distributed data base environment than any competitive minicomputers.

- The subject of cloning the PS/2 has been overworked in the
  press, but several things are clear:

  - It is not as simple to clone as the PC.

- There is no assurance that any clone will be able to run the OS/2 Extended Edition, which will be used to implement the tightly integrated data base and communications products that are planned. (Unspecified bits in the MicroChannel present some difficult problems for reverse engineering until it is known how the software will use them.)

- The masked queen has provided a sinister peek behind the mask for potential clone makers. She leaves no doubt about what she intends to do with such mates—she intends to devour them with lawsuits.

Despite much bravado among hardware vendors at all levels of the processing hierarchy, major vendors are probably aware of the problems that could be posed by SAA. Unfortunately, it is not so clear that they understand the more serious problems presented by distributed data bases. However, there is a flurry of activity to form meaningful relationships among various hardware-software vendors. Two are worthy of specific comments:

- Perhaps the oddest couple to emerge is the Digital Equipment and Apple duo. It would appear that Digital was looking for a workstation and Apple was looking for a file server, and they decided each had what the other wanted. It is difficult to believe that Digital is interested in off-loading any significant work to Macintoshes or that Apple is interested in having any significant work (such as desktop publishing) absorbed on VAXs. In fact, both probably will continue to compete, developing their own particular "solutions." (It would have been a true stroke of genius if Digital had taken the Apple II and supported it as an office workstation riding off VAXs—but I am not getting paid for that kind of advice.) Whatever the purpose, it does not appear that either company understands IBM's distributed data base strategy very well. For example:

  - Are they seriously considering integration of their systems software with common DBMSs?

  - Is Digital going to support the MAC interface and HyperCard?

  - Is Apple going to support VMS?

  - Are the two of them going to support a common version of UNIX?

The list could go on, but it doesn't take long to realize that they have just let themselves in for an SAA-size headache—if, in fact, this combination is directed toward combating SAA and IBM's distributed data base strategy.

Perhaps they are just "hanging together" so they don't hang separately. Desperate people do desperate things, but Digital and Apple shouldn't be that desperate—one can only conclude that they are confused.

• On the other hand, Tandem does understand distributed data bases, and the acquisition of Ungermann-Bass makes a lot of sense. It really helps when both your hardware and software were originally designed to support the environment in which you are (and will be) competing. Everyone at the Distributed Data Base Management Ball should admire and respect this attractive couple.

Tandem has seen fit to acknowledge that a three-tiered network is necessary by announcing "mainframe" computers along with the observation that whoever "controls the data controls the customer." It has also been reported that Tandem now believes that "distributed data bases don't work." I trust they mean that distributed data bases don't work in a two-tiered environment—I could have told them that.

While a good case can be made that IBM's distributed data base strategy may "benefit" the user and be a boon to software vendors who are smart enough to understand what is going on and flexible enough to take advantage of the opportunities that will appear in the distributed data base environment, it is difficult to see many advantages for hardware vendors. Regardless of short-term results, IBM is assembling the ultimate weapon in the competitive wars. If it works, everyone will have to do things IBM's way; if it doesn't, the myths of the "information age" will self-destruct in an antitechnological backlash.

9.3   FROM THE PERSPECTIVE OF THE COMMONWEAL

The commonweal of which I speak is composed of ordinary, run-of-the-mill citizens who do not consider themselves part of the great computer/communications revolution that is to lead us into the information age. They range from free spirits and serious artists to skeptical educators, politicians, and corporate executives. They are usually people who find time to extend their reading beyond the vast array of books, publications, and articles that extol technology. For example, perhaps they read:

- "John Naisbitt's Clip Joint" by Emily Yoffe (*Harper's*, September 1983). In this article Ms. Yoffe explored the phenomenon of Mr. Naisbitt's book *Megatrends* by exploring the underlying "methodology" used by The Naisbitt Group (TNG) in identifying trends for both *Megatrends* and the various "trend reports" that are produced as a service. The results were enough to make anyone skeptical.

  − TNG stated that it had a "data base" of 2 million articles from 6,000 newspapers and that the data base was growing by 20,000 a month. It was discovered that:

  − TNG doesn't do the clipping, but relies on an outside clipping service that is highly selective in taking only a few "interesting" articles from each paper. (The typical user of the clipping service is a high school student doing a paper on something.)

  − Since an essential element of TNG's "content analysis" is to measure the number of articles on specific subjects to establish trends, the research base is flawed from the very beginning.

  − Ms. Yoffe then explored TNG's analysis of the data provided by the clipping service and found that:

    • The "analysts" had no particular education or experience that would qualify them to analyze the trends in the broad areas (e.g., one 23-year-old sociology major was responsible for tracking developments in agriculture, consumer affairs, energy, environment, and housing).

    • The analysts themselves admitted that the methodology was "sort of vague in a sense" and that there was no real training procedure.

    • In addition, the "data base" was not computerized, but was rather the microfiche provided by the clipping service. No historical analysis was economically possible, and even the "trend reports" themselves were not indexed.

  − For some reason, Ms. Yoffe questioned the value of The Naisbitt Group's information and even had the audacity to subtitle her article: "There's a Megatrends reader born every minute," the implication being that Corporate America was being taken in by a modern-day Barnum.

- Ms. Yoffe is a skeptic. She questions the quality of data, information, and knowledge. It is embarrassing that few analysts in the computer/communications industry see fit to raise similar questions about such issues.

Mr. Naisbitt has also come out with *Megatrends 2000*, which has been serialized in at least one major newspaper. I understand it has a practically spiritual tone and is "pro-feminist." Perhaps Ms. Yoffe can be encouraged to review this latest effort. However, I doubt that Mr. Naisbitt would fare much better the second time around, even with his new-found, more intuitive view of the world.

- An editorial titled "A Lemon Dumped," which appeared in the *Times Tribune* in Palo Alto, CA, on August 29, 1985. It discussed the York anti-aircraft gun, which cost the government $1.8 billion over an eight-year development period, only to fail miserably during even the simplest tests after going into "production." Among its problems were the following:
  - The computer system tended to malfunction, especially during hot or cold weather.
  - It couldn't hit even easy targets. In one test, when programmed to shoot down helicopters, it fired on the blades of an exhaust fan in a field latrine. Now that brings us to the question of expert systems and the disturbing thought that Sgt. Alvin York of World War I fame, after whom the thing was named, might never have been able to program a computer, but he certainly would have known the difference between a helicopter and a privy—a distinction substantially less subtle than those associated with most of the knowledge-based systems we are attempting to build.
  - The editorial concluded that "among those most relieved to hear the news [that the York had been scrapped] are the soldiers who would have been 'protected' by this high-tech lemon."
- In 1988, about Bank of America getting out of the trust business because it put a computer program into operation that could not

keep track of interest payments. This resulted in yet another $60+ million write-off for what was once the world's largest bank, but which has now been reduced to a shadow of its former self because of a series of embarrassing systems failures in the "decision support" area.

In September 1988, *Computerworld* published "The Premier 100," a list of companies that supposedly use information systems most effectively. Bank of America made the list despite the fact that it was at the brink of insolvency because of systems failures. In desperate straits, BoA brought back its former CEO, who proceeded to turn the company around. In 1989, the second "Premier 100" list came out, and BoA (which was once again profitable) failed to make the list. It was also in 1989 that BoA started sending out handwritten notes of appreciation to new customers who established even modest lines of credit with the bank. The final quarter of 1989 was the most profitable in the company's history. There is a message here for the information systems industry and for CEOs everywhere.

Yes, just a little reading outside of the computer/communications trade press is enough to make skeptics of us all.

If IBM succeeds in its distributed data base strategy, there is some possibility that we may proceed at a reasonable (albeit expensive) pace toward the true benefits of computer technology. The public good is best served by orderly progress toward the information age.

If IBM fails, the skeptics will turn to cynics quite rapidly, and the partial solutions that abound will soon be revealed for what they are— extremely high-entropy systems solutions that require ever-increasing amounts of human energy to keep them from descending into chaos. The public good is not served by such systems.

9.4   FROM A REASONABLY OBJECTIVE VIEWPOINT

While I am not naive enough to think that IBM has altruistic motives for solving the distributed data base problem, I do acknowledge that it has provided leadership in the development of the technology that makes this possible. System R and System R* were research projects that cost substantially more than the effort that went into the discovery of superconductors. Competitors have been content to implement partial solutions employing these research efforts. IBM's distributed data base strategy will go beyond these efforts to develop an "industrial-strength" solution for real-world problems that exist, or are anticipated, in IBM's customers' environments. The company is being bet on SAA—not to satisfy Wall Street financial analysts or to save IBM executives' jobs, but in anticipation of the systems problems of the 1990s. I wish them well.

10

DDB Progress Report

10.1 DB2 2.2

DB2 2.2 was announced in early October 1988. It represented a modest but essential step toward distributed data base management in the SAA environment. When DB2 2.2 became available, it provided enough functionality to provide homogeneous multi-site read and single-site update within the DB2 mainframe environment (see Figures 7.1 and 7.2). This capability enabled DB2 users to read from several sites and update one of them, and it eliminated the need to collect tapes to update a DB2 site.

The DB2 announcement was significant because it ensured referential integrity. (Referential integrity exists when all relationships present in the database are understood and properly maintained by the DBMS.)

Figure 7.2 presented the concept of distributed function based on difficulty. It is possible to translate difficulty into timing, and I will update this figure (Figure 10.1) now by substituting some dates along the difficulty axis. The dates are "best case" based on my vision of how the heterogeneous operating environments should fit together. Earlier I isolated the AS/400 product as the key element in distributed data base management. Indications are that IBM does not share my view. That means that the industry may have another SNA on its hands and that Level 3 functionality may be extended past the turn of the millennium.

10.2   AS/400 AND PS/2

When IBM announced the AS/400 as the follow-on to the 3X product line in 1988, it met my expectations that it would have the architecture

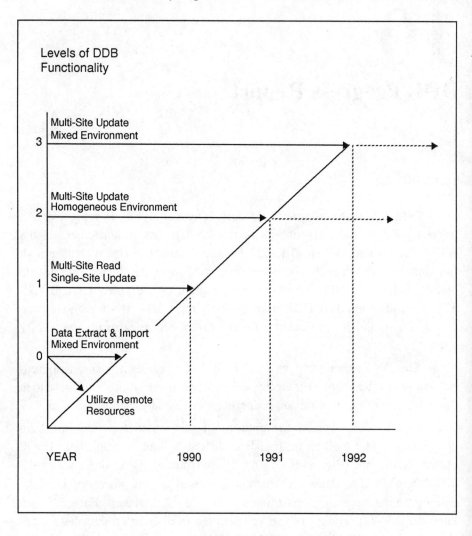

Figure 10.1 – Revised Distributed Function

Source: Killen & Associates, Inc.

of the System/38 and the ease of use of the System/36. I recommend that IBM customers and competitors familiarize themselves with the AS/400. The hardware-software architecture can provide insight into what is required for distributed data base management.

From the point of view of distributed data base management, the AS/400 has significant advantages:

- 48-bit addressing, which reportedly can be extended to 64-bit and which provides a single-level storage view that could encompass data distributed on even the largest networks. The System/370 continues to go through various "extended architectures" as the result of "networks developing more rapidly than IBM anticipated."

- Built-in relational data base management and embedded inverted list-based access mechanisms. Subfile processing provides the developer with increased development and maintenance productivity and with substantial improvements in performance. The combination of the two is important. If the user need not concern himself about where data reside in a distributed data base environment, he should also not have to concern himself with how queries are processed. The relational model (especially the JOIN command) does have inherent performance problems. The AS/400 architecture has built-in optimization tools that should at some point permit the development of a truly intelligent network operating system that would provide the performance necessary for distributed data bases.

- Advanced peer-to-peer networking (APPN) and advanced program-to-program communications (APPC or LU6.2) are integral parts of OS/400. The AS/400 has adopted a layered operating system, which I feel is absolutely essential for a distributed data base environment in which network management and data base management will be so tightly integrated that they are indistinguishable. System/370 operating systems do not have this advantage at the present time (see Figures 9.1 and 9.2). Essentially, the AS/400 with OS/400 is better architected for superior "connectivity" within its homogeneous level than is the System/370 (Figure 7.1).

- After more than two years of speculation and controversy about the Micro Channel Architecture (MCA) of the PS/2, some analysts are beginning to understand what should have been apparent all along—that the MCA will facilitate two-way communication among PS/2s and other intelligent devices on the network. The trade press seemed fascinated with the thought that "intelligent peripherals" could "seize control" of the MCA. In other words, the MCA can accept priority interrupts for data transfer. This, of course, is precisely what is required if microprocessor-based systems are ever going to graduate from personal computers to becoming integral parts of either local- or wide-area networks—and that is what distributed data bases are all about.

• The problems associated with distributed data bases when approached from IBM's traditional, highly centralized, mainframe-oriented approach become practically impossible to solve when one starts to consider the thousands of intelligent workstations that may have "owned data" that must also be shared. If minicomputers did not exist, they would have to be invented to make DDBs manageable. The AS/400 and PS/2, and their operating systems, are architected to work together in what will eventually be a tightly integrated DDB environment. System/370 hardware-software systems were not designed for this environment—they are too complex and too expensive.

10.3 IMAGE PROCESSING

Since the AS/400 arrived, IBM has also announced ImagePlus, which was heralded by the trade press as IBM's "plunge into imaging waters." Remember that when I talk about DDBM, I interpret *data* as "anything that is stored on a computer." One reason that distributed data are inevitable is because of image processing. Even with ISDN, the storing of voluminous image files off-site will not be very practical compared with the advantages of putting the file cabinets as close to the users as possible. To date, "office automation" has emphasized the production of paper, and now the current craze for facsimile will spread it more rapidly. My analysis of image processing concentrates on the storage and management of what were previously paper documents. Eliminating—not producing—paper is going to be the cost justification of the computer/communications networks of the 1990s.

Some brief comments on ImagePlus:

- I believe the AS/400 should be IBM's primary driver for image processing — the electronic file cabinets should be located at the departmental level. Therefore, when ImagePlus was announced for the AS/400, I felt it made a lot of sense. I even managed to develop a little enthusiasm until I looked at it. (It is definitely too little and perhaps even too late.) When I looked at it from a strategic point of view, I began to be concerned.

- ImagePlus was announced by IBM's Enterprise Systems Division (the large mainframe guys), which is supposed to have the expertise in marketing such complex integrated systems. And while system configurations on the AS/400 can start as low as $200,000, IBM also proudly acclaimed that the systems could go as high as $15 million when supported off a 3090 mainframe.

- Something is wrong here. I suspect it has something to do with the mentality that would still process text on a mainframe if personal computers hadn't come along to set up the Apple cart. Mainframes don't need new, inappropriate applications like image processing. Such applications will only speed their demise because there isn't much market for $15 million file cabinets.

- More importantly, this type of mainframe mentality is certainly capable of resisting the distribution of conventional data bases from mainframes. In this case, the schedule for DDBM systems (Figure 10.1) could be extended substantially.

10.4 ARCHITECTURE VS. CONSTRUCTION

It is possible to have a wonderful blueprint and all the best materials and still construct a monstrosity. A wonderful example of this exists in Washington, DC. The White House is flanked by the Treasury Building and what is now the Executive Office Building. The Treasury Building is the oldest government building in Washington (naturally), and it has a plain granite austere exterior. When it came time to build another building for the rest of government (State, War, etc.) on the other side of the White House, it was decided to build one with the same "plan" as the Treasury Building. Go to Washington, DC, and look at the monstrosity that is the Executive Office Building—it is dirty brown and adorned with exterior columns that serve no functional purpose. But—the internal floor plan is the same as that of the Treasury Building!

Then, of course, even when one attempts to build a duplicate with the same plans and materials, it is possible for shoddy workers to build an inferior building. We have all seen this happen on major systems projects. Given the same design, schedule, and comparable resources (in terms of person-months), the results can vary over an astounding range.

I am afraid that IBM may suffer from both problems in regard to SAA, and specifically to DDB.

- The SAA architecture may become cluttered with extraneous components that were not originally included in it but are now listed as "participants" (such as IMS/DC and CICS/VS). These do not add much to the original architecture—they are thrown in for those who like useless columns on buildings.

- There are certainly those who feel that the AS/400 is an unnecessary appendage to SAA because of the glorious System/370 architecture. IBM would probably announce a "PS/370" with sufficient power to be a departmental processor and distributed data base "server" if other developments at the workstation and low end of the mid-range were not already sufficiently confusing its customer base. IBM always has a tendency to offer its customers competing and confusing solutions. (I am thinking specifically of the 9370 and AS/400 models and the AIX RS/6000.)

- The statement that *DDB management and network management will become one* implies close communication between those who build data base management systems and those who build communication systems. Looking back to the 8100 (from the communications side of the house) and the 4300 (from the data processing side), there is little indication that the computer and communications sides of the IBM house understand each other very well. In fact, IBM may not understand communications very well (otherwise it wouldn't have bought ROLM).

- There are also signs that IBM doesn't know how to market the AS/400 in anything except the small business market from whence it came, and in similar configurations — dumb terminals and all. There are long customer lead times on implementation of distributed data bases, and IBM is not providing sufficient direction for its customers to be able to plan.

- In summary, it is possible that regardless of how promising SAA appears and how good the AS/400 may be, SAA may be another dose of the Chinese water torture when it comes to DDBM. As one ex-IBMer stated early on when we were discussing our analysis of SAA, DDBM, and the AS/400: "Yes, I agree with you, but they can always find some way to screw it up."

10.5   THE DANGLING QUESTION OF PROGRESS

Because of demand for AS/400s, I am afraid that the progress of DDBM will be slow. (If IBM could have met its business objectives, it would still be selling tabulating equipment.) If DDB progress is slow, the AS/400 will not assume its proper functional role within the SAA hierarchy rapidly enough to meet my "best case" forecast (Figure 10.2). The AS/400 market has enough cream that requires skimming that the Level 3 functionality could be shoved out to 1994.

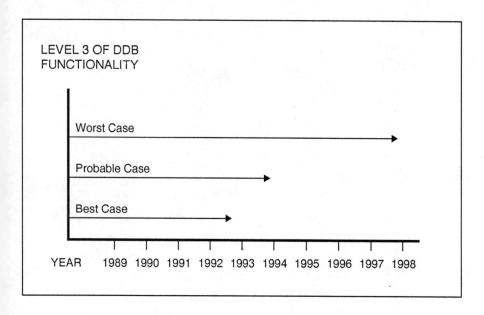

Figure 10.2 – Revised Level 3 DDB Functionality

Source: Killen & Associates, Inc.

Various "analysts" continue to consider the AS/400 a "replacement box." Unfortunately, IBM has predictably continued to sell it that way, and it still has not been "homogenized" into the SAA architecture.

If IBM attempts to establish DDBM exclusively across System/370–PS/2 operating environments, effectively ignoring the proper role of the AS/400, the DDBM effort will fall under the weight of mainframe overhead expense. Redirecting the distributed data base effort will shove out the date for Level 3 functionality to 1998. This means that, effectively, IBM would have failed to meet its customers' requirements in the 1990s. I hope this will not happen.

Therefore, the possibilities for achieving Level 3 functionality are those presented in Figure 10.2. IBM has a blueprint; it has allocated resources — it is now a question of how committed the construction workers are to making it happen.

11

Developments of Significance

The primary objective of SAA is to improve information quality and bring order out of chaos. Therefore, any critical analysis of SAA must summarize the nature of the chaos that developed during the 1980s and must assess whether developments since SAA was announced have done anything to bring order out of that chaos.

To some degree, chaos is inherent in the computer industry, but IBM must also bear responsibility for a substantial portion of it. The inherent chaos results from rapidly changing computer hardware technologies and shorter product cycles. Systems software doesn't keep up with hardware, and applications software doesn't keep up with systems software. By the time old applications systems are "converted" or new applications systems are developed, it is time to start over again with new hardware-software systems.

Customers and consultants throw up their hands in horror about the high cost of maintenance over the systems life cycle, but the high cost occurs primarily because enormous resources have been expended chasing the latest vendor hardware-software "solutions."

11.1 THE CHAOS OF THE 1980s

The computer industry is like a fox hunt where the hounds (problems) are seldom able to catch one fox (vendor solution) before another is released and runs off in another direction. The poor hounds become tired and confused. In the unlikely event that they are lucky enough to get one of the foxes holed up, the old dogs will keep the fox holed up for a long time because it is too much work to catch another one.

Vendors' end-user solutions proliferated in the 1980s. The situation degenerated to the point where it was difficult to remember the original purpose of new technology—to have problems find solutions. Now, "solutions" abounded and were beginning to find problems. Thus, some solutions became problems, and many problems started chasing their own tails.

The constant running to keep up with technology degenerated into chaos when the business environment embraced PCs during the 1980s. Knowledge workers began to distribute data in an uncontrolled fashion. Using application programs such as Lotus 1-2-3 and WordStar and data base programs such as DB2, they created data bases everywhere. No one person or group controlled the creation of these distributed data bases, and from an information systems point of view, chaos proliferated.

IBM had always believed that it could control the acceptance of new technologies among its customer base. During the 1960s and 1970s that was true. Computing was simpler, and IBM's dominance in the computer market was greater than it is now. By controlling each new release of SNA, for example, IBM controlled the marketplace's acceptance of centralized networking. Most customers could not embrace any form of networking until IBM was ready for them to have it. But by the 1980s, IBM had lost much of its ability to control the introduction of new technology.

When IBM realized the impact that PCs and the distribution of data were having, it was too late to put the genie back in the bottle. It is one thing to take a technology away from competitors, but to take technology away from emancipated users without replacing it with better technology is quite another. Unfortunately, IBM was unable at that time to offer customers anything better. The PCs, distributed data bases, and chaos were here to stay.

IBM contributed to the chaos that developed. It began to compete against itself with 9370s, System/3Xs, 8100s, and PS/2s. Even the terminology got out of hand. Distributed processors, small business systems, cluster controllers, departmental processors, servers, you name it — they were all directed toward similar applications areas. IBM's attempts to control the positioning of minicomputers in hierarchical networks resulted in more solutions than there were problems.

IBM has normally been the only company to thrive on confusion in the commercial data processing market. Mainframe customers have continued, out of necessity, to "grow" their installed applications. Small business customers and first-time users have found System/3Xs highly usable for practical business applications. IBM understood commercial customers and their propensity to select IBM whenever there was fear, uncertainty, or doubt. For IBM, creating confusion has usually been a highly effective tactical maneuver.

Therefore, during the early 1980s, IBM continued to thrive despite an increasingly chaotic environment. By the mid-1980s, however, even IBM was losing credibility among its customers. At that point, the customers (as John Akers so delicately put it) "hit IBM in the head" by refusing to chase the latest "solutions" with sufficient vigor to satisfy either IBM or Wall Street analysts. Only then did IBM realize that it needed to bring order out of the chaos it had helped to create.

11.2 SAA AND CHAOS

SAA is IBM's answer to chaos among its customer base and in the industry. SAA addresses:

- The timely implementation of applications systems by establishing common user and programming interfaces—graphics interfaces and application-enabling tools. (The objective is to improve the usability of computer systems so that user problems and applications solutions rendezvous before the user problem changes and/or before vendors come up with new hardware-software "solutions.")

- The clarification of fully supported IBM hardware-software platforms (MVS/ESA, VM, OS/400, and OS/2 EE), and the effective integration of these platforms into "networks of systems." (By narrowing the bewildering choice of IBM hardware-software "solutions" and assuring portability of applications across platforms, IBM assists users in information systems planning and decision making.)

- The fact that installed competitive systems must coexist with SAA (at least for a while) and must support established and emerging communications standards and "open networks of systems." (By accepting the reality of users' investment in "other" hardware-software systems, IBM has endorsed standards that will permit loose integration with the SAA world — a world in which some peers will be more equal than others.)

Therefore, simply stated, the purpose of SAA is to get users to implement new applications rapidly and to integrate those applications with existing applications systems into complex networks of systems.

As I emphasized previously, my analysis of SAA concluded (1) that the key to the success of SAA is distributed data base management and (2) that distributed data base management and network management will become synonymous and synchronous. Otherwise, networks of systems (and SAA) will merely increase entropy and speed up chaos.

11.3 PROGRESS TOWARD ORDER?

In reviewing what has happened since SAA was announced, I will concentrate on the implications for distributed data base management and systems integration rather than on the "usability" factors designed to stimulate sales of computer hardware-software systems. In other words, is IBM progressing toward bringing order out of chaos?

11.3.1 The AS/400

I stated earlier that sufficient demand for the AS/400 among its traditional customer base of small companies could tend to slow IBM's progress towards DDBM and toward bringing order out of chaos.

In the last three years, the AS/400 has been successful in several regards:

- It has been successful in the market. In the first five months after its announcement, the AS/400 generated $5 billion in revenue for IBM. Despite repeated predictions that this was pent-up market demand and would soon slacken, the AS/400 generated $12 billion in revenue in 1989.

- It has been successful in blunting — if not destroying — the penetration of the midrange commercial market by other minicomputer vendors. In fact, by 1990, Stephen B. Schwartz (general manager of IBM's Application Business Systems) was saying that the reason other midrange vendors were embracing UNIX was because their proprietary systems couldn't compete with the AS/400.

- It has been thoroughly successful in confusing "analysts" on Wall Street, in market research firms, and in the trade press who simply don't know what to make of the AS/400 and keep waiting for it to fail. In fact, as late as December 1989, one such expert in *The New York Times* sagely recommended that IBM "should spin off its AS/400 line" because "while the line enjoyed initial success when it was introduced in 1988 by encouraging IBM's existing minicomputer customers to upgrade, that business is now exhausted."

- And in 1990, the AS/400 generated $14 billion, approximately equalling the world market for UNIX computers. In 1992, depending on the economy and how well IBM markets the low-end AS/400s and the AS/400s with optical storage, the AS/400 might generate $17 billion.

So, as I feared, the very success of the AS/400 has slowed the progress of SAA in bringing order out of chaos among IBM's customer base. Before he left Application Business Systems for his new position (in which he will drive quality throughout the entire IBM Corporation), Stephen Schwartz admitted that the AS/400 has not moved toward SAA as rapidly as many would like. Application Business Systems is too busy selling, building, shipping, and installing AS/400s in traditional environments where there was never very much confusion in the first place. And IBM was not motivated to position the AS/400 as the centerpiece of a distributed data base strategy that would bring some order to the chaos.

The AS/400 stands in the center of, and apart from, the complexity in the mainframe hardware-software above it and the chaos of the competing desktop "solutions" below it. There are those, both within IBM and outside, who think that the AS/400 is not going anywhere because there isn't much frenetic activity around it. They are the ones who cannot recognize order in chaos even when it exists and who cannot distinguish between a real applications solution, the mumbo jumbo of all that is MVS/ESA, and the hype of the PC hucksters.

One thing is certain: by 1991, over 120,000 AS/400s were installed worldwide. Almost all of those systems are used for commercial requirements—essential business applications. Those customers represent the leading edge of SAA among the IBM customer base. They perform essential business applications, and they stand out like beacons of order in the chaos of the computer industry. They are not going to be replaced. They are not going to fade out. They, and their architectural follow-ons, will survive as points of reference and integration for "networks of systems."

11.3.2 ImagePlus

ImagePlus is a series of products that enable customers to replace paper-based systems with electronic-based systems. Electronic filing is an important aspect of office systems, which to date have tended to produce unmanageable volumes of paper documents.

Systems like ImagePlus enable companies to take a step toward the elimination of paper in the office. However, it is critical that customers implement a system like ImagePlus only after they have determined what the future requirements and processes of their company will be. Automation should always be designed to meet a company's future requirements as well as existing ones. Proper planning for image processing will ensure that companies reap the benefits of a step up in function.

ImagePlus will create new demands on customers to improve their ability to manage distributed data. ImagePlus also pushes IBM to develop distributed data base technology.

When IBM first announced ImagePlus, the company stated that it was a strategic product. To be strategic, an IBM office automation product must take customers in the direction of SAA. SAA is clearly IBM's commercial computing environment for the 1990s and beyond. When IBM first announced SAA, it stated that SAA's initial applications target was "office systems."

The initial ImagePlus product contained few SAA components. ImagePlus for the 370 was based on IMS, not the SAA DBMS—DB2. The initial ImagePlus was also based on the PC-DOS user interface, not the SAA OS/2 CUA. Many of the components of ImagePlus, such as optical disks, juke boxes, and scanners, came from competitive vendors. And, the initial ImagePlus product was developed outside of IBM's normal product development process. ImagePlus was definitely not a strategic product.

By 1990 however, and even more so in 1991, ImagePlus evolved into a truly strategic product—one that will have great impact on all aspects of data within a company. IBM announced ImagePlus products based on SAA's DB2, the AS/400, and the PS/2, and announced its own optical storage product.

11.3.3 OfficeVision

Because IBM stated that SAA would first address office systems, the arrival of OfficeVision in May 1989 should have been quite an occasion. Unfortunately, it reminded me of the old song by Miss Peggy Lee — "Is That All There Is?" Of course, the answer to that is no; OfficeVision begins to address important usability issues across SAA platforms. My disappointment in it, once again, stems from a fundamental lack of clear direction as to how these platforms are to be integrated for distributed data base management.

OfficeVision continues to demonstrate the schizophrenic view that the IBM world is divided between the sacred 370 architecture (MVS/ESA and VM) and that strange AS/400. Both sides of the IBM world will cooperate with OS/2 workstations and be wrapped in common user interfaces, but cooperation between the "hosts" remains minimal. It appears that IBM deliberately downplayed the AS/400 in the announcement. When IBM vice president Earl Wheeler (the nominal father of SAA) reportedly states: "Cooperative processing will offer users more functionality, and it will require more mainframe MIPS and storage, so everyone wins," I become very nervous.

Evidently IBM customers feel the same way. Tying LANs into mainframes so that personal computers can "cooperate" in performing simple office functions (such as electronic mail, word processing, and calendaring) has not encouraged many end users to go back into bondage. And OfficeVision isn't enough to encourage very many VSE customers to upgrade to an SAA-approved platform either.

OfficeVision is essentially a two-tiered network architecture—LAN to host. It has not yet addressed the effective integration of centralized data processing with local office systems at the work unit level. Nor has it addressed the distribution of data from mainframes to minicomputers. That would require a three-tiered distributed architecture, which still seems to be under an IBM corporate anathema.

11.3.4 UNIX and the Other World

The confusion surrounding UNIX is not IBM's fault. The blame for this one rests squarely on AT&T, the federal government, and the trade press.

IBM's position is quite clear. There are two worlds—SAA and everything else. If existing competitive systems must coexist with the SAA world, IBM would like to simplify connectivity so that customers do not have to delay installing SAA. Therefore, UNIX (whatever version) has been recognized as the operating system of choice for the other world.

This other world encompasses all the market areas in which IBM lacks the strength of its commercial market—scientific and engineering applications, the government, and the academic world. IBM sees the recognition of UNIX as an opportunity to connect to and penetrate this other world by weakening the hold of major minicomputer competitors who have proprietary operating systems. And IBM can do this with some confidence that UNIX will not seriously penetrate SAA commercial territory.

IBM has numerous reasons to feel confident about this, but I believe the following analysis of UNIX from one of the most respected research organizations in the United States sums it up best:

> Such open systems cannot ever be made secure in any strong sense; that is, they are unfit for applications involving classified government information, corporate accounting, records relating to individual privacy and the like.

That quote comes from the AT&T Bell Laboratories *Technical Journal*, Volume 63, No. 8, October 1984, "UNIX Operating System Security" by F. T. Grampp and R. H. Morris.

The preponderance of hackers prosecuted for breaking and entering have made UNIX-based systems their victims, which seems to substantiate the accuracy of this assessment. The Air Force and AT&T must be aware of UNIX security problems, since the first hacker sent to jail was cited for breaking into UNIX systems operated for the Air Force by AT&T. However, this did not stop the Air Force from being bullied into placing a major order with AT&T for UNIX-based systems after this break-in occurred.

What is scary about all this is that hundreds of hackers are breaking into UNIX systems all over the world, and the really good ones don't get caught because the installations being violated seldom talk about it.

There should not be much confusion among commercial customers about the applications appropriate for UNIX. The security problems are well known and are now beginning to receive publicity. You can be sure that IBM will be happy to clarify any confusion its customers may have about which applications are appropriate for SAA and which belong in the other world. Look for IBM to start emphasizing the "sanctity" of data.

UNIX and RISC technology are certainly driving down the cost of workstation MIPS. That is beneficial. However, tightly integrated distributed data base management matters far more than low-cost MIPS. The contrast between the order of the SAA world and the chaos of the UNIX world will become more pronounced during the 1990s.

11.3.5 RISCs, ASICs, and RS/6000

There are those who are convinced that RISC architectures combined with UNIX will blow away the commercial midrange and will seriously affect mainframes as well. IBM's highly regarded RS/6000 has already been labeled an "AS/400 killer" by some. In other words, there are those who think IBM has played Russian roulette with a fully loaded revolver. These conclusions are based on the mistaken assumption that MIPS ratings provide a meaningful measure of commercial application performance across hardware-software architectures. They do not.

There is no question that high-performance processors are needed in the commercial environment — especially for image processing, where scanners, high-resolution displays, and pattern recognition will gobble up all those wonderful MIPS and then some. However, as a data base server (as opposed to file server), the AS/400, with its integrated DBMS and communications capability, will compete against a hardware architecture (RISC) that leaves the burden of performance up to systems software developers. And current RISC architectures are not especially well suited for moving data around and sorting them, which is what commercial work is all about. The cost of such software development in terms of dollars, time to implement, and performance will be substantial for RISC-based workstations and servers, and only after this is done will meaningful price–performance comparisons between the two architectures be possible.

On the other hand, where heavy processing is truly required, there is no reason a CISC or RISC coprocessor cannot be incorporated in the AS/400 data base server. (IBM will eventually have to increase the channel capacity.) What is more likely is that processing power from application-specific integrated circuits (ASICs) will be distributed and embedded in intelligent peripherals (scanners, displays, or even specialized workstations). Ironically, CAD (computer-aided design) applications for RISC workstations will probably facilitate the designing of ASICs, which, in turn, will compete against the general-purpose RISC workstations.

However, there is no question that turmoil currently exists among workstations and minicomputers. Technology is changing rapidly, and complex changes must be made. In this regard, one thing is certain—commercial users do not like change. They do not like to change languages, operating systems, or hardware; and they fear the unknown. Current AS/400 (and System/3X) customers will not flock to the RS/6000 even if it has the IBM logo on it. They will not be confused enough to plunge from order (one might even say inertia) into chaos.

On the other hand, those IBM customers who need high-performance workstations for technical requirements—CAD, CAP, and integer and floating-point arithmetic—will rush to the RS/6000. Many of these companies will attach the RS/6000s to their 370s and AS/400s. However, here the transfer of data between the SAA systems and the RS/6000 will be limited to file transfers.

11.3.6 AD/Cycle and the Repository

AD/Cycle and the Repository are worthy of discussion in any work on distributed data bases. Unfortunately, what has been announced thus far leaves an awful lot to the imagination.

However, it is possible to make some comments:

- The "programming problem" is as old as computers. The "solution" has always been just over the horizon — macro assembly programs, FORTRAN, COBOL, PL/1, DBMSs, 4GLs, structured programming, the relational model, methodologies, applications generators, software engineering, information engineering, etc., have all been touted in their time as final solutions to the problem.

- As Fred Brooks of "mythical man-month" fame stated upon being exposed to the mysteries of programming after leading the relatively sheltered life of a computer architect: "We seem to have more terms than concepts here." "Terms" have never solved the problems of getting computers to do what we think we want them to do. The more "terms" we have, the more problems we seem to have.

  The latest "term" is CASE. AD/Cycle and the Repository are IBM's implementation of what has been referred to as C-CASE (for component CASE). Essentially, this means that all "solutions" can be rolled into a single package and "managed" so that they will work together (or at least communicate). It comes complete with all the latest terminology—entity relationship, object-oriented programming, data encyclopedia, etc.

- The most complex problem most chief information officers (CIOs) soon will face will be to understand what CASE is and which CASE components to use. (Using AD/Cycle and the Repository is like moving my "fox hunt" to the San Diego zoo and turning all the animals loose.)

- The "solutions" to the systems development problem have a disconcerting propensity to add to the mass of the problem. However, one thing is certain: the "programming problem," in both a specific and a general sense, will still be around through the 1990s and beyond.

So much for the general usability problem.

However, what we currently know of the Repository offers hope for the management of distributed data bases. It is obviously a necessary step in the right direction.

Unfortunately, C-CASE, by giving users great flexibility and a wide choice of tools, increases entropy. To maintain any semblance of order, more energy must be put into the development of the Repository, and potential users must expend more energy identifying information among the noise of alternative solutions.

Announcing AD/Cycle with three major IBM "business partners" (Knowledgeware, Index Technologies, and Bachman) only complicated the situation. Will the Repository discriminate against the vendors and users of other tools? (Knowledgeware seemed to think it had an "inside track" and ran full-page ads to exploit the IBM connection. That Fran Tarkenton always was a scrambler.)

On the other hand, Synon, Inc. (the primary CASE vendor for the AS/400) found that AS/400 customers didn't even understand what CASE was supposed to do for them. Perish the thought, but maybe most of them don't need CASE.

Giving additional flexibility and choice to the selection of systems development and methodology only stirs up more confusion. If you put a group of IS executives in a room and start talking to them about SAA,

AD/Cycle, and the Repository, you will probably become the focus of instant catatonic stares.

11.3.7   IBM Business Partners

IBM's increased dependence on "business partners" appears to be a good idea gone awry. I won't bother to trace the history from System/3X through the PC and Microsoft connection to the current state of affairs; however, while IBM's reliance on software business partners may have made sense at each step along the way, it significantly exposes IBM to dangers — including loss of reputation and possible litigation — in areas such as value received, strategic control of software directions, and account control.

The explanation for my concern (and I think IBM should be concerned also) would be worthy of a separate book. As far as this book is concerned, the point is that these software business partners are seldom, if ever, interested in seeing that SAA (and tightly integrated distributed data base management) really works. In fact, one might say that practically all of them have diametrically opposed interests. Just a few simple examples will suffice:

- MicroSoft is not really interested in seeing OS/2 EE succeed. Its efforts to promote Microsoft Windows attest to that.

- Knowledgeware is not interested in seeing IBM receive a full set of its own integrated CASE tools, or the Repository succeed in attracting component vendors. (It is only interested in taking out full-page ads showing that it has an inside track with IBM and everyone else might just as well forget it.)

- Oracle is busy advertising that it has "SAA now." This not only is misleading in the marketplace but is just not so. Oracle doesn't have a DBMS for the AS/400, and it never will have—it has a vested interest in killing the AS/400, and so does every other DBMS vendor.

- Some IBM business partners have products (and levels of service) that do not meet IBM standards in the marketplace. Some products do not perform as advertised, and some lack a good reputation among knowledgeable users. Unlike hardware products, software products are extremely difficult to test — especially in the complex web of systems software that is needed to integrate networks of systems. (Users will begin to question IBM's intention and direction in establishing some of these business partner relationships.)

- While some IBM customers may still believe that IBM is the safe choice because "IBM will make it work," they are not confident that IBM will "force XYZ company to make it work."

- When confronted with the failure of a critical business system that fails because of an IBM business partner's component, who is the customer likely to sue?

This complex web of business partners is causing confusion in the marketplace at the very least, and it could create chaos when it comes to fixing responsibility for the complex systems that will be installed in the 1990s. It is likely that only lawyers will prosper in this type of environment.

11.3.8   Artificial Intelligence and Artificial Information

We all need to become more aware of artificial intelligence and artificial information. In Chapter 5 of this book, I described data, information, and knowledge at some length. Later, I will also describe how increasing amounts of information become data to be managed. I believe that the knowledge that will be absorbed by artificial systems will take two forms: artificial intelligence, knowledge-based or expert systems; and artificial information, the result of computers "talking" with one another. It is important, for several reasons, to distinguish between these two types of knowledge replacement:

(1)   Unlike artificial intelligence, which will knowingly be integrated into systems, artificial information will come with the territory. If complex networks of systems are to be managed in the true sense of the word, artificial information must be built into the network.

(2)   Artificial information will tend to have a life of its own. A mainframe computer will "tell" my workstation that I now have certain data that I requested. These data will, in many cases, have lost any link with a responsible human source. However, I must be able to rely on them when I generate conventional information because I can't possibly verify them daily.

(3)   In addition, the system will observe me and will generate artificial information about my performance and behavior. Whether "ob-

serving" a clerk to improve her/his productivity, or "observing" an executive for "abnormal" behavior as part of system security, our systems will look over our shoulders and "tell" other systems and humans things about our behavior.

(4) Artificial information is distinguished from artificial intelligence because it is a byproduct of the data management function. Vendors will (and must) build artificial information into network operating systems. Users control the introduction of artificial intelligence by determining which domains (applications) an expert system will address.

(5) The potential for error in (or misuse of) artificial information is enormous. Humans at all levels will be asked to depend on and trust their vendor's artificial information systems. In fact, humans may not be asked — they may find themselves subordinated to artificial information whether they like it or not.

It is important to understand the role artificial information will play in the integration of data, information, and knowledge. Artificial information is going to become a fact of life during the 1990s, whether we like it or not. SAA and distributed data base management make that inevitable.

12

The Long Road to DDBM

12.1 IBM ANNOUNCEMENTS IN SUPPORT OF DDBM

It has been four years since IBM announced SAA. Considering that some major components of IBM's data base strategy (IMS and CICS) have been around for nearly three decades and that the relational model was being worked on twenty years ago, four years may not seem long, but I must confess that the road toward DDBM under SAA still looks long and rocky.

Figure 12.1 presents the milestones we have passed on this weary journey, which may be summarized as follows:

- March 1987 — The introduction to the SAA announcement included the CPI for Database. IBM gave DB2 and SQL/DS as examples of implementing products.

- April 1987 — OS/2 was announced.

- September 1987 — The "SAA Common Programming Interface — Database Reference" became available.

- June 1988 — SQL/400 was announced.

- October 1988 — IBM introduced SAA access to distributed relational data through the CPI. Two types of access were defined:

  - Remote Unit of Work (RUW)

  - Distributed Unit of Work (DUW)

IBM included a statement of intention saying that RUW and DUW would be supported in all SAA operating environments.

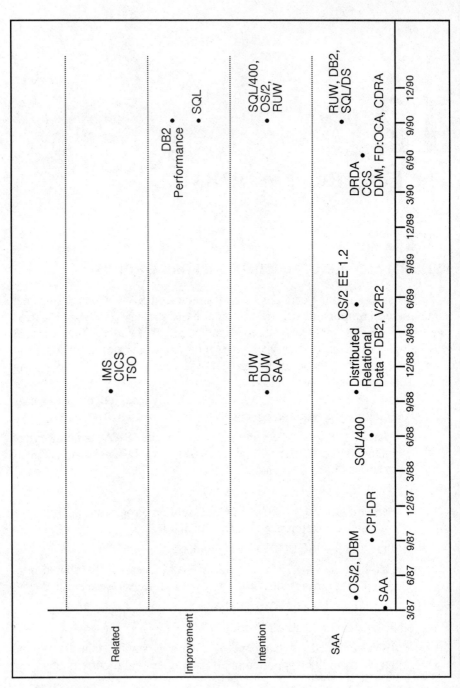

Source: Killen & Associates, Inc.

- October 1988 — Concurrently, DB2 (Version 2, Release 2) was announced with the following capabilities:
  - An application on one system could read from multiple systems.
  - From within a unit of work, a single system could be updated (a single local or remote from TSO and Call Attach Facilities, but local systems only for IBM and CICS transactions).

  This DB2 support was characterized as partial implementation of DUW.
- May 1989 — OS/2 (Extended Edition 1.2) was announced with support for RUW access between OS/2 systems.
- June 1990 — The SAA Distributed Relational Database Architecture (DRDA) was announced. It introduced extensions to SAA CCS to provide RUW access to distributed relational data. DRDA is defined as "the connection architecture that defines the flows and interactions for remote DBMS processing." Three related architectures were introduced to support DRDA:
  - Distributed Data Management (DDM), Level 3
  - Formatted Data: Object Content Architecture (FD:OCA)
  - Character Data Representation Architecture (CDRA)

  DRDA defines an architecture for other DBMSs (and file systems) to connect to the SAA world.
- September 1990 — DB2 (Version 2, Release 3) and SQL/DS (Version 3, Release 3) were announced with their implementations of RUW access based on DRDA. A statement of intent for SQL/400 and OS/2 to implement RUW based on DRDA was also issued with this announcement.
- September 1990 — IBM also announced Level 2 of SAA CPI for Database, which included extensions to the SQL language to support RUW access, and other SQL improvements (e.g., referential integrity).

The details of these milestones reveal that IBM is, in fact, considerably sensitive (especially from the lordly perspective of Enterprise Systems) to its customers' requirements for DDBM and to the complexity of the problems associated with DDBM.

But there are still some problems with IBM's perspective.

12.2   COMMENTS ABOUT THE LONG, ROCKY ROAD TO DDBM

12.2.1   RUWs, DUWs, and Missing Units of Work

Early on, along the road to DDBM, IBM defined RUWs and DUWs. I feel it is helpful also to define a missing unit of work (MUW). A missing unit of work is one that IBM has not completed in its DDBM strategy. Let's review some as they appear in IBM announcements.

12.2.1.1   MUWs 1 and 2 — Support of RUWs

According to IBM, its RUW permits "access to a single, remote relational Data Base Management Subsystem (DBMS) within a unit of work. A unit of work consists of several related SQL requests. The remote DBMS processes these related SQL statements and will update the data base only when all the statements in the unit of work have been completed successfully."

When IBM defined RUW, it used the Remote Relational Access Support (RRAS), which was available in SQL/DS, as an example of RUW access, and concurrently announced DB2 V2R2, which supported RUW. It also stated that it intended to "implement remote unit of work access from an SQL application in any SAA environment to relational data in any SAA environment."

MUWs 1 and 2 obviously support RUWs for SQL/400 and OS/2 EE.

A typical local/remote warehouse example, in which an item is not in stock in one warehouse but can be automatically located and shipped from another warehouse, was used as an application for RUW access. This is precisely the type of application for which many S/3Xs (AS/400s) are being used—building distributed applications was, and continues to be, much easier with the AS/400 architecture.

12.2.1.2   MUW 3 — Unit of Work Coordination

IBM defined a DUW as one that permits "access to multiple relational DBMSs within a single unit of work. An application program will be able to read and update data from any number of DBMSs within a unit of work. However, the operands of a single SQL statement must refer to data from a single DBMS. The application program need not know whether the data is [sic] local or remote. The DBMS will determine the location of the data."

The October 4, 1988, announcement then went on: "To provide data integrity when more than one data base is to be updated, unit of work coordination is required. A process such as two-phase commit will be required."

MUW 3 is an IBM implementation of an appropriate process for unit of work coordination.

I do not underestimate the difficulty of this technical problem. At least IBM has acknowledged that the problem exists.

12.2.1.3 MUWs 4, 5, . . ., n

IBM then stated that it intends to implement DUW access from any relational SAA environment to any relational SAA environment. It should be obvious that every time IBM issues a statement of intent, it announces MUWs.

At this time, more is missing in SAA DDBM than is available. It is a long, hard road we are trudging, and I do not want to discourage anyone by continuing to point out the MUWs. At least IBM is on the right road and acknowledges the difficulties involved. No other vendor can make that statement.

12.2.2 A Problem Peculiar to IBM (and Its Customers)

IBM and its customers have a peculiar and complex problem of coordinating the systems software that is in place under MVS/ESA. The problem stems from the evolution of data base management over the last three decades.

When IBM announced DB2 V2R2 in October 1988, the distributed data base support highlighted the following RUW and DUW capabilities:

- Read from multiple sites under TSO, Batch, IMS/DC, and CICS
- Support for updating a single local or remote site from TSO and Batch, and updating a local site from IMS/DC and CICS
- Access to a single site by a single SQL request

My comment is that coordinating and integrating DB2 with existing software (and data bases) under MVS/ESA is more complicated than interfacing DB2 with the outside relational world. I do not know how much effort IBM's systems programmers put into maintaining the mighty kludge that is MVS/ESA, but it must be horrendous. However, the real problem is that several generations of IBM systems programmers have grown up in this environment and feel that this complexity is necessary and desirable. This can lead to fuzzy thinking when applied to the outside world (whether other SAA platforms or UNIX). One example of this was a flurry of activity to make CICS available on the AS/400, the justification being that it would improve transaction processing performance. That is dangerous thinking. The last thing we should do is spread the MVS/ESA complexity disease to other platforms.

12.2.3 OS/2 Extended Edition 1.2

OS/2 EE 1.2 provided RUW access between OS/2 systems. The Database Manager enhancements were outlined as follows:

- The Database Manager supports X.25 connectivity as provided by the Communications Manager. This provides support for the Database Manager Remote Data Services between OS/2 workstations connected to an X.25 network.

- The SQL/QMF facility supports the download of data from DB/2 and SQL/DS and has been enhanced to provide the ability to specify automatic table creation and automatic import of data at the time the command is issued.

- The screen definition and layout of Query Manager menus and panels functions have been enhanced, as has enabling the execution of panel actions from Query Manager procedures. This allows more flexibility in the design of custom applications.

I would comment that the level of complexity of OS/2 EE 1.2 would be daunting even to experienced systems programmers, let alone managers of end-user computing. A "Memory Estimating Worksheet" indicates that 12.75 Mb of memory could be required for a distributed data base environment before taking into account OS/2 applications and data. DOS, Microsoft Windows, and UNIX are going to look awfully good unless there is some compelling reason to consider distributed data base and unless some imaginative cost benefit is provided.

Once again, DB/2 and SQL/DS are mentioned, and OS/400 (along with SQL/400) is ignored. (That is just another MUW encountered along the road.)

12.2.4 SAA Distributed Relational Data Architectures

Finally, on June 26, 1990, IBM straightened the long, rocky road a little bit, and we can better glimpse where we are going. The official IBM abstract of SAA Distributed Data Base Architectures reads as follows:

> Today, IBM introduces extensions to the SAA Common Communications Support (CCS) that provide the architectural basis for remote unit of work access to data distributed across an enterprise. These advanced communications protocols provide an architected solution for managing distributed relational data that resides in Common Programming Interface (CPI) to provide a new level of Procedures Language capability. A key element of Level 2 is native language support for stream input and output.

The CCS extensions are as follows:

- The Distributed Data Base Architecture (DRDA)
- New level of Distributed Data Management (DDM) Architecture
- Formatted Data Object Content Architecture (FD:OCA)
- Character Data Representation Architecture (CDRA)

The CPI extension was Level 2 of the REXX procedures language.

The benefits listed for the CCS protocols are important, and I will comment on each:

- End users or application programs can easily access information in relational data bases from any SAA system or any non-SAA system that implements DRDA in the enterprise. Information can be delivered whereever and whenever needed.

  Comment: This is obviously desirable and necessary for non-SAA IBM systems such as the RS/6000. For all other systems, it is the spider's open invitation to connect to the web.

- The customer has the flexibility of accessing and using data stored in data bases on IBM mainframe systems, midrange systems, and programmable workstations dispersed across an organization.

  Comment: That certainly is what it is all about, but beware those MUWs.

• Enhanced communications support permits data to be transferred between systems interconnected across national language boundaries.

Comment: In a recently published "Networking Wish List" (*Computerworld*, 12/17/90, p. 98), multinational connectivity was rated as the least important of ten issues by users. I think this is one instance in which IBM is leading users in providing valuable and necessary support. (Either that or the market research failed again.)

• Data may be accessed from different operating systems and different computer systems, meeting current and future business needs.

Comment: This is extremely difficult to argue against. What it means is that IBM wants to establish CCS protocols and DRDA as standards.

The CCS protocols and DRDA are sufficiently important to list here. They fall into six broad categories:

(1) Object Content Architectures allow data objects (text, graphics, images) to be created in a standard format and to be easily transferred between SAA systems.

(2) Data Streams allow programs to generate output for a printer, a workstation, or another application program elsewhere in the network.

(3) Applications Services enhance the activity of the network by providing architectures that follow data distribution, document interchange, and network management.

(4) Session Services allow two applications programs in the network to establish a dialog, to communicate, and to transfer data.

(5) Network Services provide assistance in linking across the network.

(6) Data Link Controls establish communications and transmit data across any combination of telephone lines, microwave beams, fiber optics, satellite links, or coaxial cables, using local-area networks, telecommunications links, or packet-switched networks.

IBM then stated, "The new and extended CCS protocols that collectively provide the communications architectures for distributing relational data fit in these categories and relate to one another."

IBM then describes DRDA: "DRDA is a new Applications Services protocol in CCS that allows the customer to access and use distributed relational data wherever it resides in an interconnected network of host systems and programmable workstations that have implemented the SAA DRDA." In addition, DRDA extends SQL from one system to a network of systems by "prescribing" commands, data descriptors, data, objects, communications areas, and statements.

Comment: It is now possible to see why DDBM and network management must merge. Vendors of partial solutions to these problems cannot possibly prevail in tomorrow's interconnected world. IBM is really the only game in town — like it or not.

12.3 THE ENTERPRISE DATA OVERVIEW — SEPTEMBER 1990

The Enterprise Data Overview announcements of September 5, 1990, when combined with the DRDA announcement, fairly clearly present IBM's view from the top of the proprietary SAA world and the open systems world as well. There can no longer be any question that a long, long trail winds toward distributed data base management, but at least we have a general idea of where we are heading.

The best analogy I can present is the opening of the American West. IBM is definitely pioneering, and Enterprise Systems certainly seems to be the wagonmaster. It takes little imagination to place IBM competitors in the role of native Americans. However, I get a little concerned about IBM customers — the wagonmaster for the Donner party also probably talked a lot about the magnificent Sierras and the wonderful view from the Summit. Oh, well, nobody ever said it was going to be easy.

12.3.1 New Data Management Facilities

In the September 5, 1990, announcements IBM states, "To expand your ability to manage and access data across the enterprise, IBM is announcing new data base management solutions based on advanced data base management technology. The new solutions announced today are designed to expand the availability of information by providing:

- Access to distributed data
- Data management for online transaction processing
- Data base coexistence facilities
- End-user query and reporting facilities

- Systems management for data bases."

The terms "solutions" and "information" are so sadly misused in the computer industry that it makes a snake oil salesman cringe—at least the snake oil salesman sells a solution and imparts information in the true sense of the two terms.

12.3.1.1 Access to Distributed Data

Access to distributed relational data from multiple MVS DB2 and VM SQL/DS data bases was announced. IBM stated that:

- This was the "next step toward providing distributed data base management support across the four SAA platforms—MVS, VM, OS/400, and OS/2 Extended Edition (EE)."

- The "remote unit of work distributed data base solution is based on the SAA Distributed Relational Database Architecture."

- DRDA was "designed to simplify access to relational data bases across multiple operating environments," and DRDA was the basis for managing data distributed among MVS DB2 systems and VM SQL/DS systems today.

- DRDA would "provide the basis for distributed remote unit of work support for the SAA OS/2 EE database manager when distributed support to multiple data base systems is available in those SAA environments."

Comment: The MUWs for OS/2 EE and OS/400 are obviously still with us. The only question becomes whether the wagonmaster (Enterprise Systems) really understands the price those SAA participants (and their customers) may have to pay to adapt to the DRDA architecture.

12.3.1.2 Data Management for Online Transaction Processing

IBM announced new releases of the IMS/ESA Transaction Manager (V3R2) and CICS/ESA (V3R2) which are "designed to provide high performance and high availability," and pointed out that DB2 could be used with either to do online transaction processing. It goes on to warn that in specific applications where "extremely high performance, stringent continuous availability and low-cost-per-transaction are important, the IMS/ESA Database Manager fast path facilities may provide the best solution for that application."

Comment: I have long believed that any DBMS that requires a separate online transaction processing front end cannot be deemed a satisfactory product, regardless of transaction volumes. The fact is that transaction volumes grow, and customers get stuck with horrible kludges of systems software.

12.3.1.3 Data Base Coexistence Facilities

The IBM Data Propagator MVS/ESA (a horrible name if I ever saw one) is a new product that will make it possible for customers to manage the IMS/ESA DB and DB2 data bases that are part of the kludge. IBM refers to this as "coexistence" and states that it allows more flexibility in electing the data base manager that best fits the application's requirements. Its purpose is to permit the use of IMS/ESA DB data bases for existing and high-performance applications and the use of DB2 for new applications. The objective of the Data Propagator is to maintain consistent data in the hierarchical data base and the relational data base as if one logical copy of the data existed.

Comment: Data, data everywhere, and no relief in sight. The result of the complexity of IBM's mainframe data base management systems is that data entropy increases. To avoid this natural tendency to chaos, increased energy (hardware, software, and human) must be used to maintain order. The Data Propagator is designed to maintain order, but in doing so it also facilitates the proliferation of data. It is a "breeder reactor" in the sense that it both creates and solves the problem.

12.3.1.4 End-User Query and Reporting Facilities

IBM extended SQL/DS and DB2 query and reporting facilities to further comply with "industry SQL Language standards." This is accomplished by extensions to the Database Interface of the SAA CPI. Among the extensions that support distributed data base management across multiple systems are:

- A connect statement
- Coded character set conversions
- Referential integrity
- Common SQL return codes

Comment: IBM has stated that it not only supports standards but "likes" standards. I believe that this is true with one caveat—IBM prefers to have developed the standard.

12.3.1.5 Systems Management for Data Bases

IBM has stated that its strategy is "to support enterprise-wide systems management solutions for the enterprise through the IBM System-View structure and SystemView products." The key advantages claimed for the SystemView "solution" for managing data bases are:

- Data base management tools on multiple SAA systems can be accessed and controlled from one single point of control, the OS/2 EE workstation, reducing the effort and resources required to manage the system.

- A consistent end-user interface among the products enables users to learn and become proficient with many products more quickly, simplifying the use of multiple tools for day-to-day data management operations.

IBM then states, "The SystemView solution for managing data bases provides the initial step for integrating a variety of data base management tools. As distributed data base management systems evolve, SystemView and data management support are intended to evolve to provide systems management support for the distributed environment."

Comment: I think that SystemView is needed to facilitate distributed data base management, however, the conceptual (and actual) merger of network and data base management strategies within IBM is proceeding at a rate that lags market requirements substantially.

12.3.2 Miscellaneous Architectural Considerations

12.3.2.1 Architectural Accommodation

Under the heading of "Hardware Software Synergy," IBM stated that "IBM data base management systems are designed to work together with IBM processors and operating systems."

Comment: I believe that is true. Data base management systems must be designed to work in a particular hardware-software environment if, as in the case of the System/370 architecture, that architecture was not originally designed with data base management as the primary design point. Then as the requirements of data base management become clear, the hardware and operating systems must evolve to accommodate those requirements.

12.3.2.2 Integrated Architectures

Later, IBM's announcement stated that "The OS/400 Database Manager and the OS/2 Extended Edition Database Manager are integrated into their respective operating systems. Integration of the data base manager with the operating system facilitates the use of new processor and operating system functions as the technology evolves."

Comment: I agree with this statement and can only agree that it seems to be the better approach.

12.3.3 Performance

The announcement also included significantly enhanced performance for DB2. The following improvements were mentioned:

- Relational sorting in the MVS/ESA environment was improved through hardware enhancement in the ES/9000 (370).
- Join processing is improved through new and modified algorithms.
- Batch processing is helped by a new sequential detection algorithm.
- REORG and RECOVER times are reduced.

Comment: These "improvements" tend to confirm the conclusions I reached earlier about the performance of relational data base management systems. Performance of the relational model in MVS/ESA will probably continue to be a problem, though, because data will proliferate faster than mainframe hardware and software can evolve.

13

Conclusions and Recommendations

13.1 CONCLUSIONS

My conclusions about SAA and IBM's distributed data base strategy can be stated succinctly:

- IBM needs SAA to provide a common view of its diverse hardware-software offerings.

- IBM needs distributed data base management to provide this common view and to maintain the quality of data in a distributed processing environment.

- Distributed data base management is complex and has unsolved complex technical problems.

- IBM has a distributed data base management plan that recognizes the complexity of these problems and provides the potential for an "industrial-strength" solution.

- IBM's distributed data base management solution will integrate operating systems and DBMSs so tightly that its SNA/SAA network will function as a single system that views "connected" non-IBM systems as "peripherals."

- If IBM is successful in its distributed data base strategy, I believe that:

  - It will be successful in establishing IBM account control among a broad segment of the user community because it solves real problems of data quality that are being ignored by competitors.

- It will have substantial market impact on competitive hardware and software products.

I believe that IBM (1) has a carefully conceived technical solution to the distributed data base management problem, (2) has committed the necessary resources to implement the SAA distributed data base strategy, and (3) will be generally successful in that strategy.

Timing and systems performance (cost) problems are to be anticipated in the execution of IBM's distributed data base strategy, and they will cause many tactical decisions that will divert attention from the strategic direction.

IBM's ongoing reorganizations will facilitate these command decisions. Perhaps Napoleon's maxim — "Go separately, but hit in unison; that is the greatest art of strategy" — will be foremost in John Akers's mind as he sends the troops off into this long campaign.

While it is fashionable, and trite, to state that every strategic move by IBM represents both "challenge and opportunity" for IBM customers and competitors, this is especially true as it pertains to IBM's distributed data base strategy and SAA. Based on this truism, I conclude:

• Rather than "buying computers and then trying to tie them together" or "building a network and then hanging the computers on later," it is absolutely essential that users and competitors alike establish plans to effectively integrate data, information, and knowledge.

  - For users, this means a plan that considers computer/communications networks, paper systems and procedures, and, most important, the human resources that represent knowledge within the organization.

  - For vendors, it means a comprehensive plan for how their products and services will *assist* their customers in implementing these plans. (Assist is emphasized because the snake-oil peddling of "solutions" won't work with the integration of data, information, and knowledge.)

While there is no assurance that a strategic plan based on data, information, and knowledge integration will succeed, any strategic plan based on the conventional wisdom associated with vendors of mainframes, minicomputers, intelligent workstations, or networks will assuredly fail some time in the 1990s. Classic reductionism in the distribution of data doesn't work. Giving every individual a "solution" can only lead to chaos.

The opportunities for both users and vendors are based on recognizing and understanding the problems of the information age and the need for distributed data base management. As pointed out earlier in the quote from "The Unwritten Comedy," understanding problems is primarily a process of becoming familiar with the things of which we are ignorant.

13.2 NECESSARY ACTIONS

Both users and vendors must act as soon as possible to understand the problems and plan for the integration of data, information and knowledge. This book does not purport to be a "cookbook" for developing a strategy for the 1990s, but it outlines preliminary steps toward establishing such a strategy. These steps are:

- Adopt an acceptable paradigm.
- Take SAA and DDB seriously.
- Understand both SAA and DDB.
- Understand data, information, and knowledge.
- Develop a strategic plan.
- Organize to execute and monitor the plan.
- Set up a contingency plan.

13.2.1 Adopt an Acceptable Paradigm

SAA is a complex strategy for maintaining order among the complicated information systems anticipated in the 1990s. To understand and respond to this strategy, both users and vendors must adopt a paradigm that embraces the "general theory of wholeness" that was the foundation of von Bertalanffy's General System Theory. Therefore, the first thing to do is to recognize that "Square One" of the diagram I have used frequently is the outer perimeter of the diagram, not any of the individual boxes (Figure 13.1).

All user and vendor planning must be based on looking at the forest of wholeness rather than using a reductionist approach that would concentrate progressively on particular trees, then dead logs, then small twigs, ... ad infinitum. Most certainly, we do not want to deny the existence of substantial portions of the whole. For example, saying that mainframes are going away doesn't make it so.

In viewing "Square One," it is important to remember that all complex systems exhibit a tendency toward a hierarchical order, which can best be understood by repeating the essence of General System Theory. These tendencies toward a hierarchical order can be characterized as follows:

- There is progressive integration, in which the parts become more dependent on the whole.

- There is progressive differentiation, in which the parts become more specialized.

- These cause the system to exhibit a wider repertoire of behavior, but this in turn results in:

  - Progressive mechanization, which limits the parts to a specific function.

  - Progressive centralization, in which the emergent leading parts dominate the behavior of the system.

The most important dictum associated with General System Theory goes back to Aristotle, who stated that the whole is greater than the sum of its parts. Specifically, as presented by von Bertalanffy:

- The properties and modes of action of higher levels are not explicable by the summation of the properties and modes of action of their components taken in isolation. If, however, we know the ensemble of the components and the relations existing between them, then the higher levels are derivable from the components (*Perspectives on General System Theory*, Ludwig von Bertalanffy, George Braziller, Inc., 1975).

- He then summarized, "in order to understand an organized whole we must know both the parts and the relations between them."

The importance of adopting a paradigm based on General System Theory cannot be overemphasized. This paradigm is absolutely essential if we are to understand the computer/communications networking environment of the 1990s and the "information age."

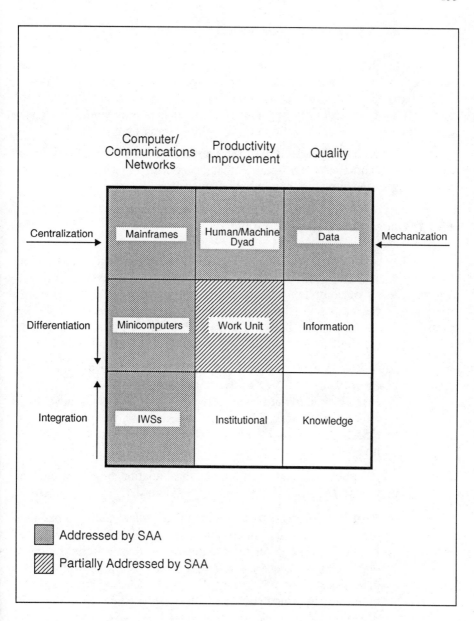

Figure 13.1 – Starting at Square One — Wholeness

Source: Killen & Associates, Inc.

13.2.2   Take SAA and DDB Seriously

In the last year, both users and vendors have begun to take SAA seriously, so I will not belabor this point. However, as mentioned previously, I expect IBM's distributed data base strategy to go through a cycle in which lack of understanding comes first, then minimization of importance, followed by the realization that something important is occurring.

In the coming years, it will be increasingly important to keep an eye on SAA and SAA/DDB—those that do so will have the best chance of building systems to empower knowledge workers.

13.2.3   Understand Both SAA and DDB

I have attempted in this and other books to aid readers to understand SAA and IBM's distributed data base strategy. However, I am dealing with levels of complexity that are difficult to describe, and I make no pretense of presenting anything more than a strategic overview of "the parts and the relationships between them." The following additional comments are appropriate as we start looking at Square One in more detail.

- IBM is addressing distributed processing and distributed data bases with SAA. Specifically, it is adopting a common view of diverse IBM hardware and software "solutions" that have been less than satisfactory. The SAA announcement explicitly stated that SAA would first address office systems and then proceed with vertical industry systems (Figure 13.1).

- Some additional comments about the "relationships between the parts" in IBM's SAA/DDB strategy are in order:

  - IBM has observed that users want to "share data" rather than distribute data. Essentially, this means that the emphasis of IBM's strategy is on integration rather than differentiation of data. This is certainly a convenient assumption on IBM's part, since it fits neatly into the traditional, highly centralized, mainframe-oriented strategy of the past.

  - IBM's priorities are pretty much as depicted in Figure 13.1.

    - Maintain centralized network and data base management on the mainframe "leading part."

- Make intelligent workstations dependent upon higher levels in the processing hierarchy (mainframes and minicomputers) network and database management.

- Proceed cautiously with the differentiation and distribution of data down the processing hierarchy.

- Mechanize the management of data as required by the preceding three priorities.

The important thing for users and vendors to understand is that, while IBM's strategy may seem self-serving in the extreme, when viewed using any holistic paradigm, it has sound technical justification.

Two other things to assimilate are that: (1) the importance of mechanization of distributed data base management does not depend on the amount of data that must be distributed, and (2) all the tendencies toward hierarchical order (centralization, differentiation, integration, and mechanization) proceed in parallel within complex systems.

Those who do not understand the challenge of IBM's SNA/-SAA/DDB strategy will not be able to avail themselves of the advantages and opportunities it affords.

13.2.4 Understand Data, Information, and Knowledge

Earlier in this book, I defined data, information, and knowledge. Simply stated, data is everything resident in computers, and IBM has a strategy designed to control computer/communications networks (SNA), systems software (SAA), and DBMSs (DDB). IBM wants to sell hardware and the SNA/SAA/DDB strategy is designed to put IBM in a strong competitive position. If you understand IBM's strategy and are willing to accept its strength, it is possible to proceed to Square Two (Figure 13.2) by simply inversely viewing Square One.

Square Two reveals that information management, knowledge management, and institutional performance are not addressed by SAA at this time, and the battleground of departmental systems (Work Unit Productivity) is far from secured by IBM. For users who do not want to be "controlled" and competitors who do not want to be overrun, the most effective immediate tactics are to concentrate resources where IBM is the weakest. IBM is weakest on some pretty high ground — the name of the game in the information age is improved institutional performance.

Before developing a plan to advance toward the high ground not yet occupied by IBM, it is important to understand some fundamental facts about the effective integration of data, information, and knowledge.

- Contrary to the popular wisdom, data (even high-quality data) do not have any intrinsic value to the institution. It is the analysis

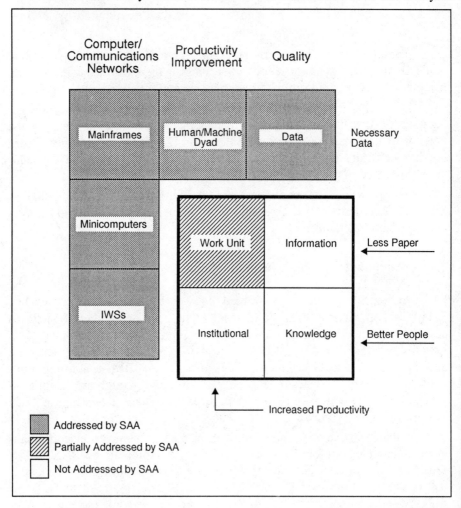

Figure 13.2 – Proceeding to Square Two — The High Ground

Source: Killen & Associates, Inc.

and interpretation of those data by knowledgeable human beings and the transactions they execute that have value.

- Also contrary to the popular wisdom, the value of information cannot be determined by its volume, how pretty it is, or how fast it is conveyed to a human being. The value of information is determined first and foremost by the quality of the human being who conveys it.

- Contrary to wishes currently popular in the artificial intelligence community, computer systems will never replace significant numbers of human beings as the primary repositories of knowledge in Square Two. In fact, the problem in the 1990s may very possibly be a shortage of knowledgeable people to develop, manage, and monitor the integration of data, information, and knowledge, so that chaos does not result from the complex systems we are creating.

When it comes to data, information, and knowledge, we have indeed been going about it all backwards. We have been installing a bunch of computers, building a bunch of networks, storing a lot of data, producing a lot of information, and dumping it on human beings. When things don't seem to work right, we decide the problem exists because the people are "dumb." Then we make the whole kludge easy to use, so we can produce more information with more complex systems that no one understands. As these systems become easier and easier to use, less knowledgeable humans produce more and more information that is of less and less value (quality). Essentially, we are building information systems "solutions" and hanging the people on later.

Rather than starting with data and increasing the flow of information on practically a random basis, we should:

- Define what knowledge is required to accomplish whatever the purpose of the institution is, and identify the human beings who either have that knowledge or are capable of assimilating it.

- Determine what information requirements are needed to enhance the value of the knowledge and the people. The more knowledgeable the people, the less information required.

- Determine what data are needed to support the people.

Simply stated, when you understand that productivity improvement starts with knowledgeable (better) people, reducing the amount of noise in the information flow (paper), and providing needed data (high quality), you will improve institutional productivity. Whether you use information systems or sell products and services, this people-oriented approach to the integration of data, information, and knowledge will help you progress toward the high ground. In other words, emphasize the basics—start by understanding the problem (knowledge) and then develop solutions, not the other way around.

13.2.5 Develop a Strategic Plan

IBM's SNA/SAA/DDB strategy requires a strategic response from users and competitive vendors. This is true regardless of the degree to which you accept IBM's strategy or its ultimate success. To do this, you must identify Square Three, which, not surprisingly, is knowledge (Figure 13.3).

Progress from Square One through Square Two to Square Three may appear to be a classic reductionist approach to problem solving, but it is not. Knowledge adds another dimension and opens up all the richness of vertical and cross-industry applications, which have infinite variety, not only among themselves, but among the human-machine dyads, work units, and institutions that use computer/communications technology to enhance productivity.

This is merely to say that we need knowledge to define data/information/knowledge requirements, and when it comes to knowledge, "experience has no substitute." Based on that bit of wisdom, we can conclude that it would be *unwise* to base a strategic plan on the following:

- Vendor "solutions" that can range from IBM's SNA/SAA/DDB down through expert systems to the latest whizbang spreadsheet package. You should not determine data/information/knowledge requirements based on the tools that are available.

- Consultants' advice that is based on either "prepackaged thinking" or academic training and/or achievement. When developing a plan for integrating data, information, and knowledge, you should be wary of consulting organizations with easily identified "solutions" (4GLs, relational DBMSs, etc.) and those with personnel who have academic credentials, but no practical experience—consulting is not a substitute for specific applications and industrial experience.

- "Glass house" information systems personnel who have specialized in fitting business problems to vendor "solutions." You can

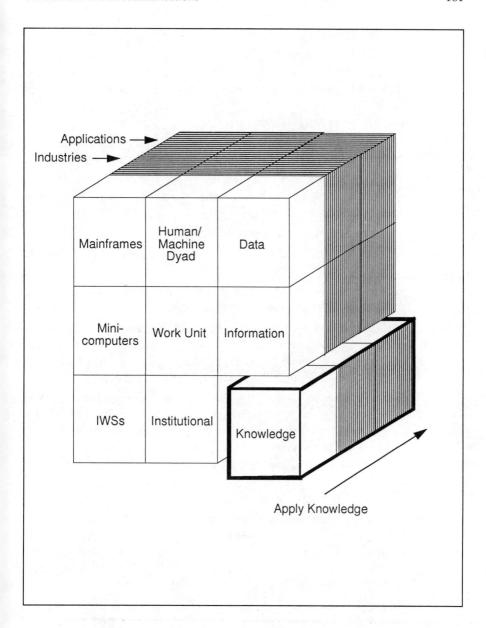

Figure 13.3 – Identifying Square Three — Depth of Knowledge

Source: Killen & Associates, Inc.

usually identify these personnel by the blue decor within the glass house.

- "Tunnel-vision" advocates of distributed processing who feel that work unit "solutions" can be easily expanded to the enterprise. You can usually identify them by the number of stones they throw at the glass house.

- "Ease-of-use" freaks who insist that computers should be made so easy to use that neither training nor experience is necessary to "get results." They can be identified in many ways:

  - They will use computers only when they can "talk" with them in natural language.
  - They believe that a spreadsheet package is a "solution."
  - They believe that "micro-mainframe links" will solve the problems of distributing data.
  - They use a "mouse" and delight in telling stories about the "programming" prowess of their ten-month-old child.

Having eliminated approximately 95% of the "experts" who are all too anxious to apply computer/communications technology without considering data/information/knowledge requirements, it is possible to provide some guidance in the development of a strategic plan for the institution.

- Get experienced, knowledgeable, operating executives involved in developing an information systems plan for the 1990s. (The use of both experienced and knowledgeable is not redundant, because while the type of knowledge required depends on experience, it does not follow that all experienced personnel are knowledgeable.) This advice applies equally to CEOs, responsible CIOs, and vendors (including consultants).

- Start with a knowledge assessment of the organization's capability and requirements. Assume that computer/communications technology (regardless of how effectively it is employed) will not be a substitute for knowledgeable (highly qualified) people during the 1990s. It is a safe assumption!

- Recognize the vendor-promoted myth, which has been accepted by all too many otherwise responsible people; that the cost of computer technology is always cheaper than that of human beings. Be aware of the possibility (I might say probability) that an expert system that can achieve results comparable to 95 percent of the "experts" may be substantially more expensive (when all the costs for hardware, software and data are considered) than hiring a human from among the top 5 percent. This caveat on the application of computer technology applies at all levels of the productivity hierarchy — much has been said about the "value" of data and information (with precious little substantiation), but cost is seldom mentioned.

- With this caveat in mind, assume that it will be technically possible to have all the data and information needed to support the institution "on line" in the 1990s. This includes archival tape files, microfiche, paper, and all those "distributed data" that were presented in Figure 7.2. Fundamentally, this assumes that IBM will be spectacularly successful in its SNA/SAA/DDB strategy.

- Next, assume that regardless of where you stand now (in terms of information systems installed or products and services offered), you will be part of the environment that will evolve according to the tendencies of General System Theory (progressive centralization, differentiation, integration, and mechanization). This assumption leads to certain "subassumptions" about the relationships of the "parts" and the flow of data/information, depending on your current orientation.

  - If data are currently under highly centralized control on mainframes, the plan will necessarily focus on differentiation and on how data are to be distributed to work units and individuals.

  - If data are currently decentralized to work units, the plan must focus on centralization for network control, integration with other work units, and differentiation to the human/machine dyad. (If it appears that minicomputers are caught in the middle, that is because they are.)

  - If data are currently distributed down to the workstation level (or are in the process of being distributed on an uncontrolled basis), the emphasis must be on integration through higher levels in the hierarchy. If that integration is to the work unit, it is possible that all the problems of being caught in the middle will have to be faced. (If it appears that uncontrolled distribution of data to intelligent workstations is a major part of the problem, that is because it is.)

- If you have already architected and established a data structure and network that satisfies your needs, recognize that the tendencies of the environment will affect you because information systems are, by definition, open systems. There are no steady-state information systems — that is the reason maintenance costs are so high. However, do not attempt radical restructuring in an effort to expedite the evolution—horrible and progressive mutants can occur.

- Finally, base the data/information/knowledge strategic plan on the capabilities of computer/communications technology without restricting the "knowledge network" to specific vendor solutions. The assumption that all information and data to support the institution can be on line suggests many exciting possibilities for the 1990s.

  - "Knowledge nodes" on the network can be established without regard for geography or organization. When users do not have to worry about where the data are, the logical progression will be that we do not have to know where the physical knowledge resides (although in both cases, we must know that they exist and what the quality is). This will facilitate all those "far-out" possibilities of tapping the knowledge of part-time employees, consultants, and information services regardless of geographic location.

  - Data may (and, in some cases, must) be moved close to the knowledge node that needs them, thus improving their usefulness in terms of availability and response time. (This can be anything from manageable distributed data bases to the physical distribution of vast data bases on optical disk.)

  - Unlike paper media, electronic media are conveniently processible by computer. There is the possibility that vast amounts of information can be screened, analyzed, and directed to the appropriate knowledge nodes — regardless of whether they are individuals or work units.

  - Technological wonders that have been considered "pie-in-the-sky" are all possible in planning for the 1990s, if we plan to use the technology rather than having vendor solutions imposed on us.

This brings us back to IBM's SNA/SAA/DDB strategy. I maintain the position that what IBM is attempting to do with distributed data base management is necessary to reap the benefits of computer/communications technology in the 1990s. However, I am very much aware that there is substantial risk of failure if IBM's entire strategy is adopted in any specific situation. The primary risks concern IBM's ability to accomplish what it has set out to do on a timely and cost-effective basis (hardware/software performance).

When looking at IBM's strategy, it is possible for both users and vendors to get the impression that IBM is trying to back them into a corner (Figure 13.1). And there is good reason for fearing that this is the case. Fortunately, if you exercise care at this phase of developing a strategic data/information/knowledge plan, it should be possible to accept the positive aspects of IBM's strategy and break out of the intended trap. By rearranging the smaller squares, we can identify Square Four and have a "foursquare" foundation for highly individualized distributed data base strategies (Figure 13.4).

Essentially, this rearrangement puts IBM in a box. It concedes IBM control of many "enterprise" systems where highly centralized, mainframe-oriented distributed data bases are truly required, but opens up competition for all those applications systems that do not require distributed data. While this may seem exceptionally attractive, and quite simple to accomplish on the intelligent workstation used to create this book, putting IBM into a box is never easy to accomplish. Before even trying to do this, you must take the necessary actions indicated in Sections 13.2.1 through 13.2.5, a formidable task which can be summarized as follows:

- Adopt an acceptable paradigm and recognize the inextricable "wholeness" of Square One.
- Take both SAA and DDB seriously. It is not a question of whether or not IBM is committed to making this happen, or whether we need distributed data bases. It is just a question of the degree to which the SNA/SAA/DDB strategy will be successful.
- Understand IBM's strategy. It will be a significant part of the information systems environment of the 1990s — that must be accepted like death and taxes.

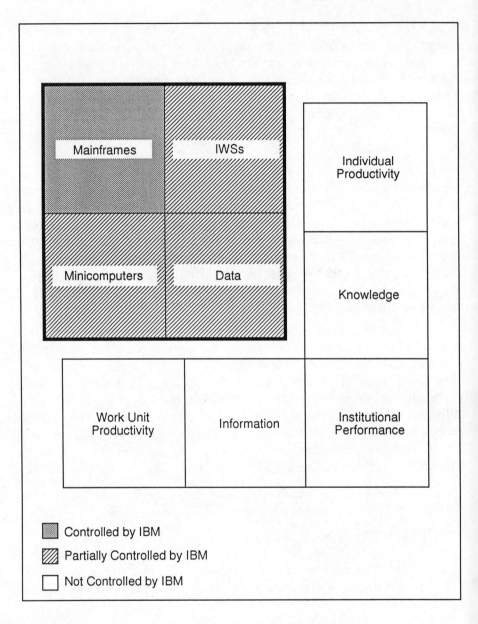

Figure 13.4 – Creating Square Four — IBM's Box?

Source: Killen & Associates, Inc.

- Understand data, information, and knowledge and how they inter-relate. Hit the high ground of knowledge and institutional performance where they "ain't" — yet!
- Develop strategic plans based on experience and knowledge that will permit seizing the high ground by applying computer/communications solutions to specific requirements rather than fitting problems to available solutions.
- Then you can think about rearranging the squares and gain some mobility of implementation for the specific applications systems you are thoroughly knowledgable about.

13.2.6 Organize to Execute and Monitor the Plan

The strategic plan for integrating data/information/knowledge, if properly prepared, will unquestionably cut across traditional organizational structures in all types of institutions. Fortunately, as pointed out in the previous chapter, there will be substantially more freedom in establishing and connecting the knowledge nodes (either individual or work unit) on the information networks of the 1990s. This will mean that both geographic and organization bounds can be crossed with relative ease. Therefore, customers as well as vendors can choose how they want to organize — traditional, hierarchical structures can be maintained and everything can be done on a project or task force basis, or entirely different organizational approaches may be taken. It is beyond my ability to predict all the forms that these may take. It should suffice to emphasize once again the flexibility and freedom that will be possible.

Having abdicated responsibility for providing specific guidance on the "necessary action" that must be taken on organization, I offer two important observations, one for users and one for vendors (including IBM). They concern the ascendancy of certain functions that have traditionally received short shrift in many organizations. In the 1990s, information network users will find it necessary to give greater emphasis to data base administration (regardless of the terminology used), and vendors will be forced to recognize the strategic importance of field service (maintenance). The following observations may prove helpful in organizing these functions:

- Data base administration has traditionally been considered grubby work and has been relegated to clerical status in most organizations. With the expanded definition of data provided in this study, and the nature of the strategic plans for integration of data/information/knowledge discussed in the previous chapter of this book, the data base administration function (while it will probably be renamed) will become the premier information systems function.

- During the development of the strategic plan, the importance and value of data will be realistically established for the first time. As more and more conventional encoded data, paper information, and knowledge are captured and made available on line, it will become increasingly important to maintain this true corporate resource and guide its use.

- The skills required for the function will increase dramatically as the systems evolve. Much of the clerical aspect of the work will be distributed to the work units, under the direction of the data base administration function. The skills that remain, and will of necessity be expanded, will embrace many current and new professions and will require librarians, experts skilled in information theory and data base structures, network planning experts, "knowledge engineers," experts in queueing network theory, and those who can apply the tools of operations research effectively to entirely new areas—all the skills required to assure the necessary management and flow of data, information, and knowledge to the other knowledge nodes within the enterprise.

- The question of whether or not applications programmers will give way to end-user-developed systems becomes moot—highly skilled experts will be needed to create, monitor, and maintain the quality of this corporate data asset and to assure the flow of necessary information. What this function will be named and how it will be organized is also moot—whoever controls the quality and flow of information in the institution assumes the power for the success or failure of that institution.

- Executive management should understand the radical changes that are possible in the power structure during the development of the strategic plan and when they organize to implement and monitor that plan.

• The foregoing comments apply to vendors as users of computer/communications technology, and I assume that the most valuable data available to systems vendors will be their knowledge of customer applications systems requirements. In addition, the era when vendors depended on the mass replacement of hardware and software systems is coming to a close. SAA may be the last full cycle of classic hardware-software upgrades that can be cost-justified. Once we begin to implement strategic plans for integrated data/information/knowledge networks, hardware-software sales will be associated with maintenance to enhance services and to maintain performance levels. We can anticipate the following:

- Even relatively large organizations will have to contract for the planning, installation, and maintenance of physical networks that incorporate a variety of equipment, software, and communications services.

- Once installed, most organizations will prefer single-source maintenance for change management, problem isolation and repair, performance monitoring and improvement, and cost control. Essentially, network operation will be turned over to an outside services company.

  [During the last year or two, "outsourcing" has become the craze. Kodak contracted out with IBM to consolidate its data processing operations. (Talk about letting the fox into the hen house!) Later, Kodak contracted out with IBM and DEC for the operation and maintenance of its network(s). (Talk about harnessing two pit bulls to the same dog sled!) Needless to say, this is not exactly what I had in mind. After stating that I did not consult with Kodak on their "outsourcing," I offer a moment of silent prayer.]

- Many of these functions were included under the "data base administration" organization for end users. While I do not anticipate that even small organizations will turn over responsibility for corporate data to an outside organization, the design, installation, and maintenance of the physical network are challenges even the largest organization would be happy to eliminate.

- In a relatively short period of time, maintenance will probably be the chief source of revenue over systems life. And, even most of the new hardware-software sales will be directly attributable to those responsible for network maintenance.

- If these observations are correct, and I believe they are, the field service function will naturally achieve new stature in vendor organizations. Exactly how significant these changes will be and how rapidly they will occur remains to be seen, but there is the potential that iron peddlers may become order takers for the full field service organizations described above.

IBM, with its extensive network of MAPs and VARs, is developing imaginative, interorganizational arrangements for essential account control functions that would have been considered unthinkable ten years ago. This trend is expected to accelerate in the 1990s and as SAA comes closer to reality.

13.2.7 Set Up a Contingency Plan

I expect that most strategic plans developed in response to IBM's SNA/SAA/DDB strategy will fall into one of several categories.

- Those that are based on the acceptance of SAA and depend on its success for implementation of their strategy. This would apply to a high percentage of large, mainframe-oriented, commercial users; applications software vendors who view SNA/-SAA/DDB as an environment that will expand the market for their products; and network product and services vendors who see distributed data base management opening up the true potential of networking.

- Those that supplement and/or complement SAA and are target windows of opportunity. Whether the plan is for a user who will depend on IBM delivering certain products on schedule, or a vendor who is attempting to establish a competitive foothold on the "high ground" not addressed by SAA, contingency plans should be made for IBM missing or improving anticipated schedules.

- Those that directly compete with IBM's SNA/SAA/DDB strategy and depend on IBM's failure in either technical development or market penetration of that strategy. It will be increasingly difficult to contain IBM within the confines of Square Four if IBM succeeds on both counts. However, specific targets of opportunity on the high ground can be identified as part of a contingency plan that calls for general retreat and fortification. (Many hand-tailored, application-to-application, pairwise connections will be relatively impervious to penetration by the general distributed data base management solution for a long time.)

Therefore, while there will be many possible contingency plans, depending on the original strategy employed, the most important advice I can give is to take the necessary actions outlined above and to monitor IBM's progress, and/or lack thereof, carefully.

13.3 ATTRACTIVE OPPORTUNITIES

The general opportunities available for users and vendors who accept SAA can be summarized as follows:

- SAA will provide the tools to begin integrating office automation with conventional data processing applications.

- SAA will provide an opportunity to address the quality of data and information (as opposed to concentration on form).

- The acceptance of SAA, and IBM's distributed data base strategy, will allow users and vendors to concentrate on the complex problems associated with white-collar productivity.

- These opportunities translate into the following opportunities for vendors:

  - For independent software vendors who have been developing applications for various levels of the processor hierarchy, potential markets automatically expand significantly as soon as they adopt SAA.

  - The markets for the development of expert systems in specific domains are just beginning to open up, and as IS departments become free to address these areas, the opportunities within these markets should improve significantly.

  - There is also a significant new applications market that specifically addresses the problems of information flow and the integration of data, information, and knowledge. (IBM is still mainframe-oriented in its thinking—this means that it is concentrating on data base management.)

- In addition, industry-specific applications represent an outstanding opportunity, with the additional incentive of having IBM as a potential customer (or partner) for the final product.
- Beyond the applications layer of the SAA architecture, there are opportunities for high-performance hardware-software systems that compete directly against SAA systems on a price-performance basis.

These are opportunities without considering the possibility of viewing the IBM SNA/SAA/DDB network as a single distributed data base management engine and isolating Square Four within Square One (Figures 13.1 and 13.4). The concept of taking the initiative away from IBM transpired during the analysis for this book. Viewed from this new perspective, the focus on the opportunities becomes even clearer.

13.3.1 Address Real-World Applications Problems

I have praised IBM's distributed data base management strategy for addressing real technical problems. However, IBM's development efforts have been unrealistic. The changing role of IBM systems engineers (they are spending substantially less time working with customers on real problems) and the increased dependence on MAPs and VARs have made IBM less sensitive to real-world applications problems. This is especially true at the minicomputer level of the processing hierarchy.

Knowledge of real-world applications problems makes it possible to determine where IBM's plan for distributed data base management is needed and where it is overkill. This will identify opportunities for establishing reachable goals for penetrating Square Four (Figure 13.5).

- The real-world applications requirements for data base management reside somewhere between the hard-core mainframe applications that employ centralized data bases and the IBM objective of having an enterprise system where the entire network looks like one system. As IBM begins to extend control of data out from the mainframe, it will provide "solutions" that exceed these requirements. To the degree that this is true, there will be opportunities for more realistic and cost-effective solutions.

- I do not think that penetrating the hard-core mainframe applications is a reachable goal for competitive vendors. While there may seem to be a lot of inefficiencies in the glass house, we should know by now that the glass is bulletproof. The off-loading of mainframes will be controlled by the owners of the glass house. The hard-core mainframe applications need "industrial-strength" distributed data base management facilities.

- However, not everyone needs an enterprise system. Some, for various reasons, will not be able to implement it, and still fewer will be able to afford it (especially the early implementations).

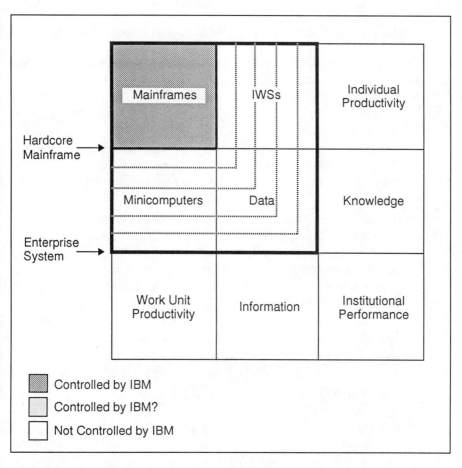

Figure 13.5 – Opportunities as Reachable Goals

Source: Killen & Associates, Inc.

• By establishing reachable goals based on real-world applications requirements, vendors may have substantial opportunities to penetrate Square Four.

IBM's ImagePlus announcement (especially the MVS/ESA version) is an excellent example of a "solution" that may be unaffordable for many IBM customers. Business partners and competitors have ample opportunity to penetrate Square Four with image processing hardware and software products, and with systems integration services.

13.3.2 Improve the Quality of Data, Information, and Knowledge

Just as the objective of IBM's SNA/SAA/DDB strategy is to create an enterprise system that controls data on a network-wide basis and, therefore, treats the rest of the world as "peripherals," it may be possible to improve and control the quality of information and knowledge and treat the IBM enterprise system as a "peripheral."

Figure 13.6 identifies Square Five, which illustrates the extraction and sharing of data among a work unit—the classic departmental processor that now begins to integrate data processing applications of significance.

• All the complexity of managing distributed data bases (where they are necessary) is handled by the IBM enterprise system. Most information does not need access to data, wherever they are, on a demand basis. For most work units, reporting (even ad hoc reporting) and query are normally accomplished against established data formats that seldom change, and most analysis and information are generated based on a specific time period.

• Knowledge about the real data requirements for specific work units shows that data can be "distributed" on a scheduled basis. Using mainframes as "virtual printers" for work units is seldom cost-effective.

• As optical disks become available for archival storage of both encoded data and paper records (depending on access requirements), distributing (publishing) such disks to work units will be substantially more cost-effective than storing them centrally. In addition, the backup of local files locally will be economically justified. Once again, "virtual disks" on mainframes will be unnecessary for many applications.

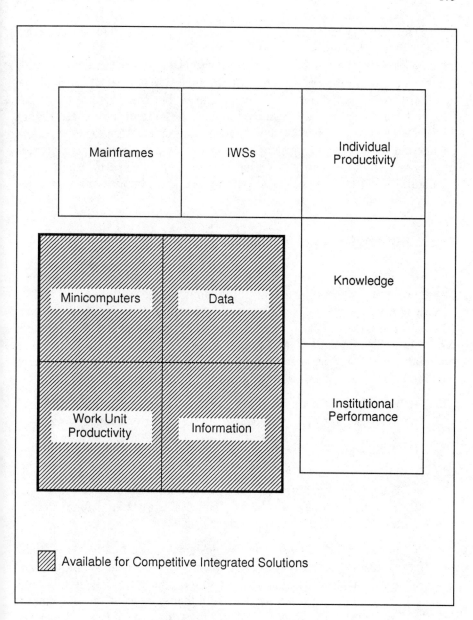

Figure 13.6 – Square Five — The Information System

Source: Killen & Associates, Inc.

The strategy of taking advantage of IBM's distributed data base management solution is especially applicable for knowledge-based systems. The need to tie these systems to data base systems has already been recognized. Since expert systems are in their infancy, it is difficult to determine how tightly they will be integrated, but the degree of integration will vary significantly with the domain the system addresses (Figure 13.7). Detailed knowledge of the specific requirements for expert systems is inherent in the knowledge engineering process. An enormous opportunity exists for those who can define and implement expert systems. The availability of DBMSs from IBM will increase these opportunities substantially.

13.3.3 Differentiate and Mechanize Functions

Hardware-software vendors probably will have substantial opportunities to differentiate and mechanize functions at the periphery of IBM's SNA/SAA/DDB strategy. I say probably because that depends on how IBM positions the AS/400. If it is "properly" positioned and supported, which in my opinion is not the case now, it could severely limit these opportunities. However, specific targets of opportunity will remain, under any circumstances, in the following areas:

- Hardware/software monitors for LANs and wide-area networks to be used for both problem isolation and performance tuning.

- Aggressive use of optical memories for both data and information storage.

- Data base machines for performance improvement of relational systems. (These could be as simple as "sort boxes" for maintaining indices internal to the system.)

- Hardware-software systems designed specifically to handle sequential batch files (yes, sequential batch). The relational purists notwithstanding, a deck of sorted punch cards is "intuitively" and practically easier to deal with than a deck of unsorted punch cards (which is what relational tables look like). Batch sequential has never gone away, and in a distributed environment, it will remain a primary means of file transmission among distributed nodes.

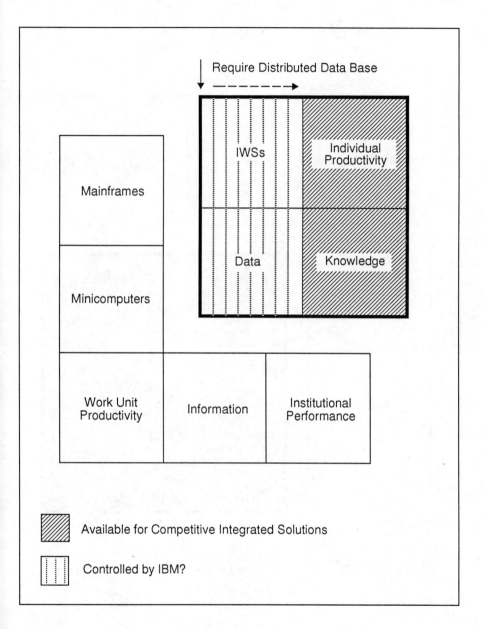

Figure 13.7 – Square Six — The Knowledge System

Source: Killen & Associates, Inc.

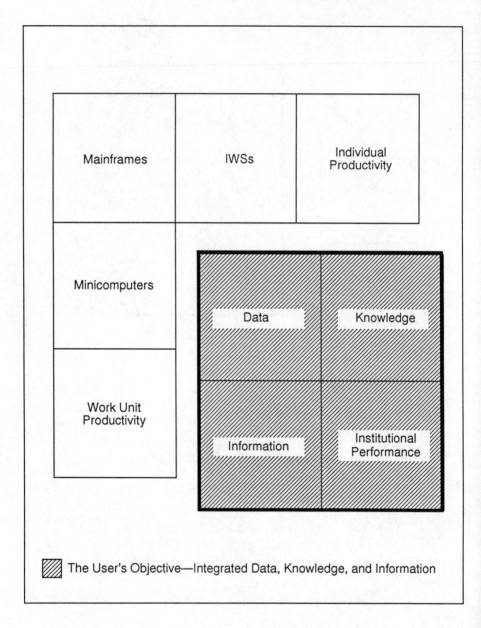

Figure 13.8 – Square Seven — The Ultimate Goal

Source: Killen & Associates, Inc.

13.3.4 The Ultimate Goal

The ultimate goal of computer/communications networks is to improve institutional performance. The ultimate challenge/opportunity for information systems management, computer hardware and services vendors, and consultants is to provide executive management with the tools and education necessary to effectively use the data/information/knowledge available to them (Figure 13.8). The opportunities for those who can do this are unlimited. It appears that IBM is addressing the potential problems of data quality that have been outlined in this book. With careful analysis and planning, both users and competitors can benefit from IBM's efforts.

Appendix A: The IBM Organization

TO MEET THE COMPETITIVE CHALLENGE

To understand the impact of SAA on information quality in a distributed environment, we must understand how IBM is organized.

Over the last few years, the IBM Corporation has made fundamental changes to its organizational structure and has reduced its head count. These changes have helped the company to meet the increasing challenges of the 1990s, but to remain competitive, IBM knows that it must be increasingly vigilant. This year the company plans to streamline its operations even more.

IBM wants to accomplish three objectives: to improve responsiveness, to sharpen competitiveness, and to increase efficiency.

In the late 1970s, John Opel introduced a plan to reduce the number of people needed to support IBM's manufacturing function. The company began to automate its factories, to use outside sources, and to increase its use of third-party sales organizations.

In the 1980s, the company continued to realign and streamline its personnel; it had approximately 387,000 employees by 1989. Between 1986 and 1990, IBM reassigned nearly 50,000 employees to developing, marketing, or supporting products. Since 1988, 15,000 employees have been shifted to the field as marketing reps and systems engineers. Concurrently, IBM reduced its U.S. plants from nineteen to fourteen.

On December 5, 1989, John Akers announced that the company would reduce U.S. head count by another 10,000+ in 1990. IBM also planned to significantly improve the productivity of its 36,000 programmers. That effort should further trim the headcount while maintaining or improving the company's productivity.

I believe that these changes indicate that IBM is addressing the competitive challenge.

TOP MANAGEMENT AND THE MANAGEMENT COMMITTEE

John Akers is Chairman of the Board of IBM and heads its Corporate Management Board. The board is supported by an Executive Committee, other committees that oversee specific business affairs of the company, and an Advisory Board that largely consists of retired IBM executives and officers.

The IBM Management Committee (MC) makes the company's day-to-day business decisions. Akers, who heads this committee (Figure A.1), is supported by Jack Kuehler (IBM's new president), Michael Armstrong, and Frank Metz.

Akers, who succeeded John Opel as chairman and chief executive officer of IBM in January 1985, had been president of the company since 1983. He held both posts until June 1989, when Jack Kuehler was named president.

Kuehler, a 33-year IBM veteran, is the company's leading technologist. His appointment as number-two ranking executive departs from the traditional IBM trend of naming a sales or marketing expert to this office.

Kuehler, who holds a B.S. degree in mechanical engineering and an M.S. in electrical engineering from Santa Clara University, joined IBM's San Jose Research Laboratory in 1958 and advanced through the IBM ranks in various technical and management positions. He assumed responsibility for worldwide development and U.S. manufacturing for IBM's technology and computer systems in 1985; then he became a member of the board of directors in 1986, an executive vice president in 1987, and a member of the Executive Committee in January 1988.

As corporate executive for IBM United States, Kuehler spearheads all U.S. manufacturing. As president, he wields slightly more power than he did as vice chairman; according to IBM bylaws, the president can *act for* the chairman, while a vice chairman *assists* the chairman.

C. Michael Armstrong was named a member of the MC when Kaspar Cassani stepped down from his committee seat and vice-chairmanship of the IBM board in November 1988. Armstrong is an IBM senior vice president and the board chairman of IBM World Trade Europe/Middle

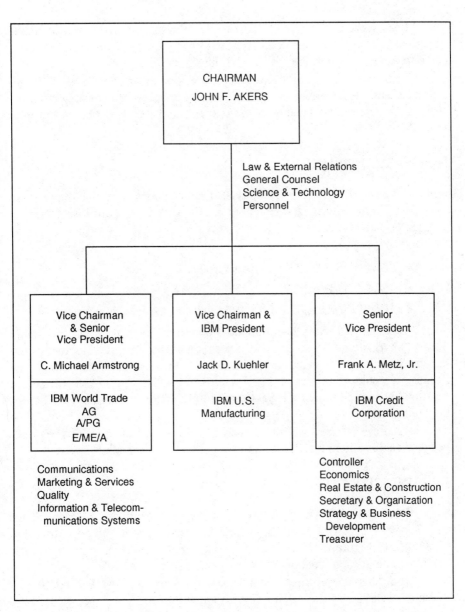

Figure A.1 – IBM Management Committee

Source: Killen & Associates, Inc.

East/Africa Corporation (EMEA). He also directs the IBM World Trade Americas Group and the Asia/Pacific Group. In 1988, Armstrong relocated to Armonk, where he reports to John Akers.

Frank Metz, a senior IBM vice president and long-time Management Committee member, manages IBM's finance, real estate and construction, strategy and business development, and the IBM Credit Corporation.

IBM WORLD TRADE

IBM World Trade encompasses four organizations that have more than 5 million customers throughout more than 130 countries. The geographic organizations are:

- IBM United States
- IBM World Trade Americas Group
- IBM Asia/Pacific
- IBM World Trade Europe/Middle East/Africa Corporation

IBM United States commands attention in this book not only because it contains most of IBM's resources—product development, and the marketing and service organization for the United States—but also because it contains Programming Systems, the LOB responsible for spearheading the development of SAA and responsible for developing distributed data bases.

Needless to say, the three world trade organizations are important because each of them distributes and supports IBM products.

IBM UNITED STATES

IBM United States has seven LOBs, including a U.S. Marketing and Services organization. These seven groups report directly to Terry Lautenbach (Figures A.2 and A.3), who reports to IBM president Jack Kuehler. The groups' headquarters are located in Somers, NY.

Upon his appointment as general manager of IBM United States, Lautenbach assumed the day-to-day responsibility for U.S. operations. Previously, IBM's Management Committee held that responsibility. Lautenbach was a senior vice president and group executive of Information Systems and Communications before being named general manager of IBM United States.

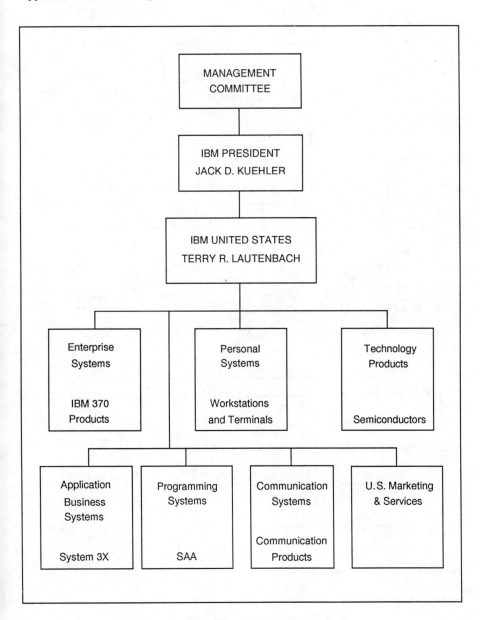

Figure A.2 – IBM United States Lines of Business

Source: Killen & Associates, Inc.

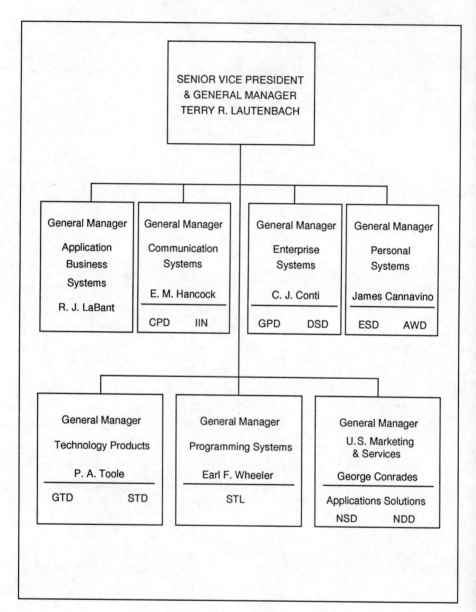

Figure A.3 – The Lautenbach Organization

Source: Killen & Associates, Inc.

The IBM lines of business and their fundamental technologies are:

- IBM Enterprise Systems: Manufactures System/370 products — including the 3090, 4381, and 9370 systems; high-end storage devices; character band systems printers and related operating systems software; and host operating systems — and controls DPPX and image processing development. Enterprise Systems accounts for more than half of IBM's hardware/software equipment revenues.

- IBM Personal Systems: Produces IBM's workstations, personal computers, displays, monitors, most printers, typewriters, copiers, publishing systems, and related operating systems software. This division is IBM's second largest in revenues, providing 18 percent of hardware/software sales.

- IBM Technology Products: Manufactures semiconductors and packaging for systems and technology products.

- IBM Application Business Systems: Concerns itself with the System/3X, the AS/400, low-end storage systems, and related operating systems software. This division is IBM's third largest organization, earning approximately 12 percent of the hardware/software revenues.

- IBM Programming Systems: Develops data management software, programming languages, and application enabling software under SAA, and some non-SAA software products, worldwide.

- IBM Communication Systems: Manufactures communications systems, related operating systems software, the S/88, and the S/1, and has responsibility for the IBM/Siemens/ROLM company relationship.

- U.S. Marketing and Services: Provides marketing and services to all lines of business across the United States.

- Application Solutions: Works with IBM customers to develop solutions for their total information processing requirements. This line of business unites application development, systems integration, professional services, and market development activities, and focuses on promoting IBM ties with companies that develop, market, and install IBM products.

Enterprise Systems

IBM Enterprise Systems, IBM's largest operation from a revenue standpoint, is headed by IBM senior vice president and general manager Carl J. Conti. Enterprise Systems concentrates on the 370-based business, which includes the 370 DASD (direct access storage device).

Two divisions report to Conti: the Data Systems Division and the General Products Division (Figure A.4).

Personal Systems

James Cannavino, IBM vice president and general manager of IBM Personal Systems (Figure A.5), replaced Robert Gerstner, who stepped down in September 1989 for health reasons. Cannavino's mainframe experience should help IBM tightly couple the SAA OS/2 and 370 products.

Personal Systems focuses on IBM's desktop systems, including the PS/2, the high-performance RT workstation, and the operating systems software and supplies. The PCs come under the aegis of the Entry Systems Division; workstations, such as the RS/6000, belong to the Advanced Workstation Division that IBM created in December 1988.

Cannavino previously headed the Entry Systems Division, which concentrates on IBM's OS/2 business.

The Advanced Workstation Division has been charged with developing a UNIX-based product line ranging from the PS/2 to 3090 mainframes.

Development Operations ensures that AIX products are highly interoperable with SAA. That technology must be in place so that the IBM sales force can promise that: (a) AIX-based systems will work better with SAA than competitors' open software systems will, and (b) customers who buy SAA can more effectively interoperate with open systems—preferably with IBM's AIX.

Technology Products

IBM senior vice president and general manager Patrick A. Toole heads IBM Technology Products (Figure A.6). Toole was formerly group executive for the Information Systems Technology Group. TP concentrates on the worldwide development and U.S. manufacturing of logic and memory technology and on the electronic packaging for the entire IBM product line.

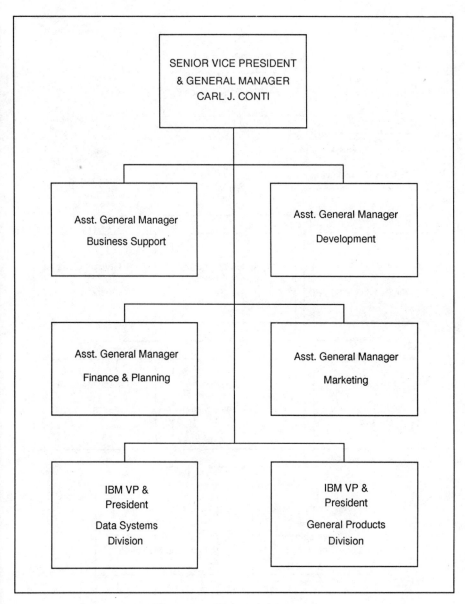

Figure A.4 – Enterprise Systems

Source: Killen & Associates, Inc.

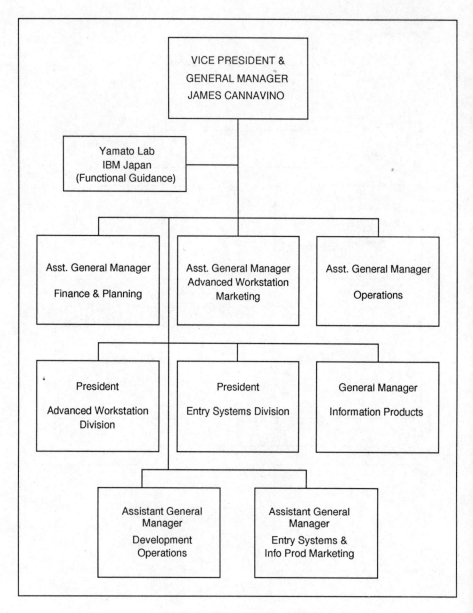

Figure A.5 – Personal Systems

Source: Killen & Associates, Inc.

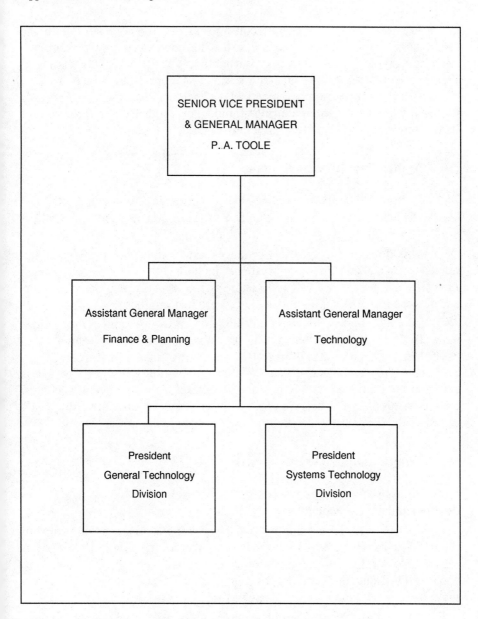

Figure A.6 – Technology Products

TP provides IBM's manufacturing and development sites with the semiconductors and circuit packaging for the company's information systems and products. (In 1988, the Burlington, VT, IBM plant became the first in the industry to produce semiconductor chips from 8-inch wafers.) The Advanced Technology Center in East Fishkill, NY, explores methods for designing and manufacturing future generations of microchips at IBM's semiconductor facilities around the world.

Application Business Systems

In May 1990, IBM announced that Robert J. LaBant, of U.S. Marketing & Sales, would replace Stephen B. Schwartz as head of Application Business Systems.

This division (Figure A.7) produces IBM's midrange processors and related software and operating systems, including the AS/400 (announced June 21, 1988) and the System/36 and System/38. ABS also develops storage devices for IBM's midrange and PS/2 product families.

In 1989, under Schwartz's leadership, ABS generated more sales than all UNIX sales combined. His organization has been extremely successful in selling the AS/400 to IBM customers (the S/36, especially the S/38, and 370 customers, especially those who want to migrate to a less complex environment), but it has not succeeded in winning new accounts. LaBant's mission will be to extract as many sales as possible from existing S/36 and S/38 customers and to find ways to obtain new accounts.

Programming Systems

Programming Systems is largely responsible for developing IBM's distributed data base technology.

Earl F. Wheeler is vice president and general manager of Programming Systems (Figure A.8), which was created in April 1988. He is responsible for the development of the SAA architecture, SAA products such as DB2 and the IBM Repository, and some participating SAA programming development projects, such as IMS.

This LOB clearly supports the existing 370 application enabling software infrastructure, which includes data base software, and develops appendices to that infrastructure, which includes all the SAA products that are needed to support the management of distributed data bases.

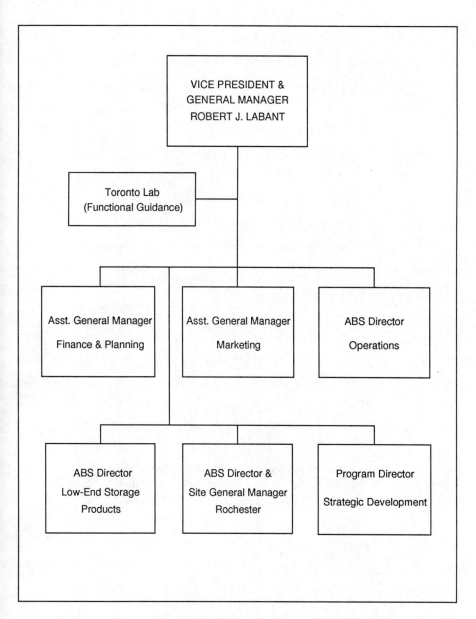

Figure A.7 – Application Business Systems

Source: Killen & Associates, Inc.

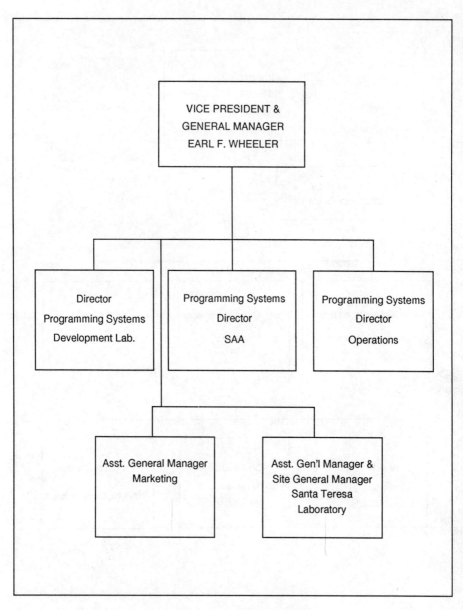

Figure A.8 – Programming Systems

Source: Killen & Associates, Inc.

In mid-April 1989, Wheeler named Tom Furey, former director of the Rochester Development Laboratory, which produced the AS/400, assistant general manager of Programming Systems and site general manager of the Santa Teresa Labs (Figure A.9). Parts of the Cary, NC, and Rochester, MN, Labs also report to Furey. The Cary Lab concentrates on languages, particularly the CSP (Cross Systems Product). Santa Teresa concentrates on 370 languages, data base management systems such as IMS and DB2, CASE tools (AD/Cycle), and AI.

Santa Teresa Labs

Santa Teresa Labs is critical to the development of software technology for customers' existing and future requirements. One of those future requirements is the management of distributed data. Santa Teresa Labs is also crucial to IBM's immediate and future revenue. IBM's revenue will continue to suffer if STL does not add distributed data functionality on a timely basis.

STL is responsible for developing three key software technologies for managing distributed data bases—relational technology, CASE, and knowledge-based systems (KBS). Relational technology is needed because it is too difficult to build applications that manage distributed data with traditional hierarchical data base technology. CASE minimizes the difficulty of developing major applications using IBM 370 software. Knowledge-based technology is needed for network and data base management, as well as for automating operations.

IBM's flagship relational product is STL's DB2. About 5000 licenses have now been sold, and an industry has developed to support it. STL continues to improve DB2's performance.

At the heart of IBM's CASE activities are the AD/Cycle framework and STL's MVS Repository. Peter Harris, president of Adpac Corporation, one of IBM's AD/Cycle associate software companies, states that AD/Cycle holds the potential of transforming programming from a hand-crafted activity to an automated process. To date, about 24 companies have agreed to order AD/Cycle and to become part of the "Early AD/Cycle Customer" program. It is much to early to say whether AD/Cycle, of which the MVS Repository and the IBM Information Model are fundamentals, will be successful.

STL's KBS technology is important to distributed data bases because of the need to manage "artificial" information.

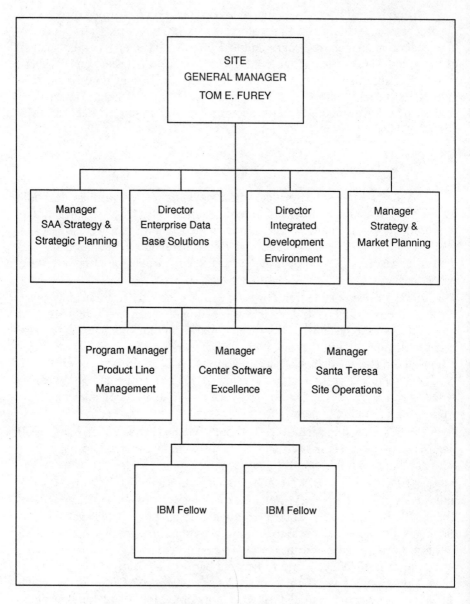

Figure A.9 – Santa Teresa Labs

Source: Killen & Associates, Inc.

STL Management Changes

In the last couple of years, STL has been rocked by management changes at the very top. In *IBM: The Making of the Common View*, I pointed out that Morris Taradalsky headed STL in 1987. In June 1988, Taradalsky resigned and joined Apple Computer Corporation.

Taradalsky was replaced by Dr. Leonard Liu, who had been managing STL's CASE developments. Liu hardly had the opportunity to warm Taradalsky's chair before he resigned and joined Acer—a Northern California company, backed by Taiwan, that clones IBM PCs.

The loss of two STL general managers in such a short time raised a lot of questions. I suspect that the ramping up of SAA and the 1988 reorganization that pulled STL out from Enterprise Systems and made it part of Programming Systems played a major role in the reshuffling.

The loss of these two general managers did not negatively affect IBM's ability to develop distributed data base technology. It is well known that large development projects and organizations have a life of their own, independent of efforts to "manage" them. While turnover of key personnel at the working level will usually adversely affect schedules, changes at the executive level seldom have an immediate effect unless the new executive cancels the project.

Liu was immediately replaced by Tom Furey, an executive from Kingston, NY, who had SNA experience, but who had no 370, 370 distributed data base, or SAA experience.

Furey's last assignment was the development of the AS/400, and there have not been many winners in IBM — politically, technically, and financially — like the AS/400 for a long time.

While directing the AS/400 development, Furey's objective was to adhere first to the needs of the 3X follow-on customers, and second to the objectives of SAA. At STL, Furey supports Earl Wheeler's plan for developing the SAA environment. We expect that Furey will lead STL for a few years and then move into a position at Purchase or Armonk.

Communication Systems

Ellen Hancock, formerly president of the Communication Products Division (CPD), is vice president and general manager of IBM Communication Systems (Figure A.10). She was promoted to this position when Terry Lautenbach became president of IBM United States. Hancock is the

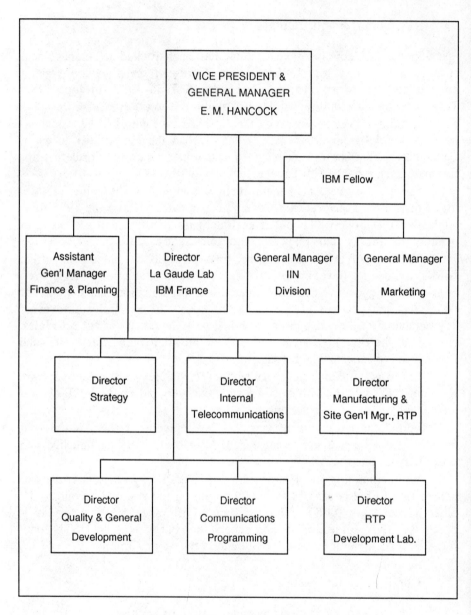

Figure A.10 – Communications Systems

Source: Killen & Associates, Inc.

highest-ranking female executive in IBM and the most prominent female executive in the world telecommunications industry. For about two years before the IBM/Siemens alliance, the entire ROLM operation reported to Hancock, who played a major role in creating the IBM/Siemens alliance.

Hancock joined IBM as a programmer in Armonk, NY, in 1966. For some time, she worked on the development of VTAM (virtual telecommunications access method). After serving in various staff and managerial positions, Hancock became director of communications programming for CPD in 1981.

In 1983, after the IBM Management Committee decided to purchase ROLM stock, Hancock advanced to vice president of communications programming in CPD. In 1984, she became assistant group executive, systems development, for the Information Systems and Technology Group, and in 1985, she joined the Information Systems and Storage Group.

Hancock first became an IBM vice president in 1985, was named vice president of telecommunications systems for CPD in December 1985, and was named president of CPD in October 1986. About this time, ROLM became part of her charter. In January 1988, Hancock assumed her present position, general manager of Communication Systems.

Hancock's responsibilities in Communication Systems are to develop Systems Network Architecture (SNA) and IBM's communications products, which include connectivity and network management software, controllers, and modems. The organization's products enable IBM products and SNA nets to intercommunicate and allow IBM products to communicate with non-IBM products and OSI networks.

Hancock's responsibility to the IBM/Siemens alliance is to ensure that IBM develops the host-based functionality to interface with ROLM Systems, and to influence the direction of ROLM Company and ROLM Systems. She is a member of the board of directors of both ROLM companies and a member of the IBM/Siemens Operating Committee, a committee of five IBM and five Siemens representatives who coordinate strategy.

Hancock is in a position to significantly affect the future of IBM and the future of customers. Her current communication systems goals include providing IBM customers with communication functionality for (1) network and systems management, (2) voice-enhanced systems, and (3) OSI, SNA, and TCP/IP networks.

(1) Network and Systems Management: Customers need more network and systems management. Hancock has ambitious plans under way to increase the functionality of IBM's network management

product, NetView. Her organization is also working with several
other IBM organizations to develop an SAA framework and product
set, along the lines of OfficeVision and AD/Cycle, that will lay the
groundwork for significant improvements in the management of
IBM systems. The new product may be called SystemsVision or Ad-
minVision.

(2) Voice Enhanced Systems: Communications Systems will add
functionality at the IBM hosts to support ROLM Systems' and other
PBX suppliers' requirements.

(3) OSI, SNA, and TCP/IP: OSI standards continue to emerge and
to become important to some customers. Communication Systems
plans to increase IBM's support of OSI standards and to extend
SNA technology. Since IBM decided to become a leader in open
software systems—UNIX—it also decided that TCP/IP support was
fundamental if it wanted to sell to the UNIX networking world.

U.S. Marketing and Services Group

The U.S. Marketing and Services Group (Figure A.11) markets and
services IBM products in the United States. Senior vice president and general manager George H. Conrades, who reports to Terry Lautenbach,
heads this organization, which handles all U.S. channels of distribution,
marketing development and support, and customer products servicing.

Application Solutions

The newly created Application Solutions line of business (Figure
A.12) reports to Conrades, providing much of the marketing development
and support function. This organization provides total solutions to customers, such as using third-party application software, integrating IBM and
non-IBM hardware and software, and providing consulting services. On
December 13, 1989, IBM named Ned Lautenbach an IBM vice president
and general manager of the Applications Solutions LOB.

IBM WORLD TRADE AMERICAS GROUP

The IBM World Trade Americas Group Board includes representatives from Guatemala, Brazil, Colombia, Argentina, Mexico, Chile, Vene-
zuela, and Peru.

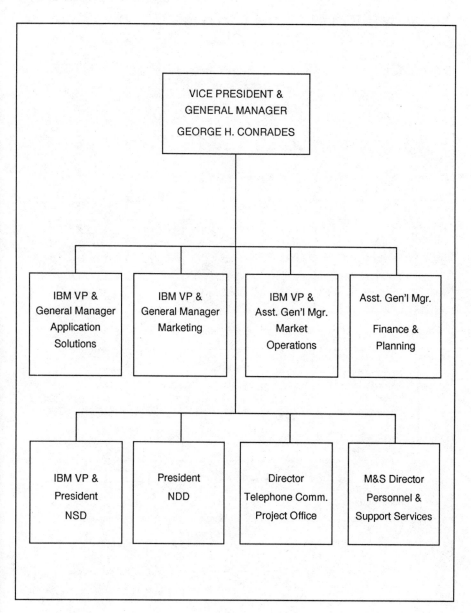

Figure A.11 – U.S. Marketing and Services

Source: Killen & Associates, Inc.

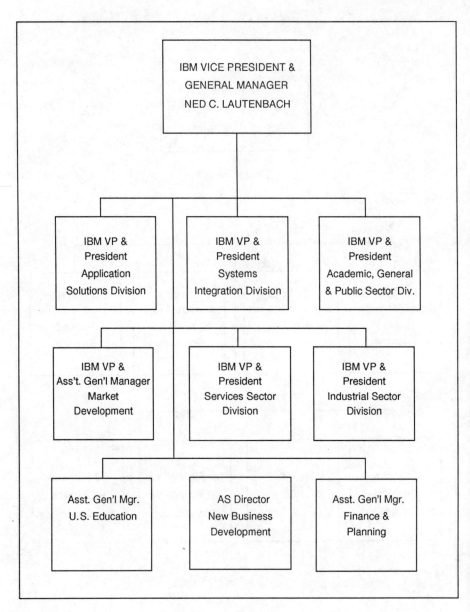

Figure A.12 – Application Solutions

Source: Killen & Associates, Inc.

To extend its global marketing efforts, IBM has created software development institutes in 10 Latin American countries within this group to promote application programs for IBM products. IBM Canada focuses on joint development programs on leading-edge technology — it now has about 75 joint projects with customers.

IBM WORLD TRADE ASIA/PACIFIC GROUP

Edward E. Lucente, vice president and president IBM Asia Pacific, heads IBM's World Trade Asia/Pacific Group. Board members include executives from Australia, Hong Kong, Malaysia, Japan, and Singapore.

Recognizing the rapid growth in information processing throughout this area, IBM is pursuing alliances here. The largest expansion to date has been in Japan—by 1990, IBM Japan had 18 alliances with Japanese companies. Other IBM installations are pursuing alliances in Taiwan, Korea, and Singapore. Twenty application development centers have also been established in countries served by this group.

IBM WORLD TRADE EUROPE/MIDDLE EAST/AFRICA

Dave McKinney, who formerly managed IBM's operating staff, is now an IBM senior vice president and president of IBM World Trade EMEA. He reports to Michael Armstrong. Board members represent France, Spain, Germany, Italy, the U.K., and Sweden.

McKinney directs operations in IBM France, IBM Germany, IBM Italy, IBM United Kingdom, and a Central, Northern, and Southern Unit. Recently, IBM Europe signed a joint venture with 10 leaders in the travel and airline industries. They will use IBM systems in a network designed to handle high-speed transactions such as ticketing and auto reservations. IBM also has alliances in Europe with Ericsson and Fiat.

OTHER IBM ORGANIZATIONS

Research Division

The Research Division, an important part of IBM (in 1988, IBM invested approximately $5.9 billion in research, development, and engineering), is less well known and less visible to the world than are the IBM lines of business. This division, which reports to J. A. Armstrong, the vice president of Science and Technology, conducts basic research and develops emerging technologies for future IBM products.

The group's research developments include advances in semiconductor technology, the extension of miniaturization to CMOS (complementary metal-oxide semiconductor) technology, the use of X-ray lithography to make advanced computer chips, and setting records (Almaden Research Center) in high-temperature superconductivity.

Research scientists also have been working on image processing technology for IBM products, and IBM researchers and University of California Davis specialists have collaborated on a robotic system for hip implants.

IBM Credit Corporation

IBM Credit Corporation is a wholly owned subsidiary of IBM that offers financing for IBM products to IBM customers. It reports to Frank Metz. Over the years it has introduced a number of leasing plans to meet customers' needs. For example, IBM's Total System Lease allows midrange customers to finance total data processing needs under one agreement; Flexible Exchange Lease allows customers to exchange leased equipment for that with new technology.

SUMMARY

I hope this overview of IBM's organization has helped readers to understand the IBM Corporation overall and has helped identify the IBM groups responsible for supporting SAA and the activities that affect information quality.

Appendix B:
IBM Programming Announcement —
March 17, 1987

IBM Systems Application Architecture

Today, IBM announces IBM Systems Application Architecture, a collection of selected software interfaces, conventions, and protocols that will be published in 1987.

IBM Systems Application Architecture will be the framework for development of consistent applications across the future offerings of the major IBM computing environments—System/370, System/3X, and Personal Computer.

Highlights

Systems Application Architecture provides the foundation for IBM to enhance the consistency of IBM software products by:

- Providing a common programming interface
- Providing common communications support
- Providing a common user access
- Offering common applications
- Enhancing the availability and consistency of National Language implementation

Description

IBM offers systems based on several different hardware architectures and system control programs. By pursuing a multiple-architecture strategy, IBM has been able to provide products with outstanding price/performance to meet our customers' requirements. Today, IBM's products support the information processing needs of people in very different environments.

IBM Systems Application Architecture makes it easier for IBM's broad product line to solve customer information processing needs by providing the framework for the development and delivery of IBM products that address consistency requirements across the major IBM systems. Systems Application Architecture provides the foundation for IBM

- To enhance the consistency of IBM software products

- To define a common programming interface with which customers, independent software vendors, and IBM can productively develop applications that can be integrated with each other and ported to run in multiple IBM Systems Application Architecture environments

- To define common communications support that will provide interconnection of systems and programs and cross-system data access

- To define a common user access, including screen layout, menu presentation and selection techniques, keyboard layout and use, and display options

- To offer common IBM applications that run in each of the major computing environments

Delivery of the IBM Systems Application Architecture will be evolutionary, beginning this year and continuing on an ongoing basis. This is the beginning of a long-term strategy similar to the process that has implemented IBM Systems Network Architecture (SNA). SNA started as a framework for consistency in the communications environment and has continued to be enhanced and extended. Today, SNA is the basis of communications for IBM's products and for many other vendors' products. In addition, IBM will continue to invest in applications and systems software that is specific to particular computing environments.

Elements of the Architecture

IBM Systems Application Architecture consists of four related elements—two of which are new (Common User Access and Common Programming Interface). The third is based on extensions to today's existing communication architectures (Common Communications Support). These three establish the basis for the fourth, Common Applications, developed by IBM to be consistent across systems. Independent software vendors and customers developing applications for IBM's major systems will also be encouraged to use IBM Systems Application Architecture products.

In addition, Systems Application Architecture provides IBM with the foundation to enhance the availability and consistency of National Language implementation in software products.

Common User Access: The Common User Access defines the basic elements of the end user interface and how to use them. The primary goal is to achieve (through consistency of user interface) transfer of learning, ease of learning, and ease of use across the range of IBM Systems Application Architecture applications and environments.

The Common User Access is a definition for IBM-developed software to adhere to over time and will be published so that customers and independent software vendors can develop programs that follow this definition.

Common Programming Interface: The Common Programming Interface is the application programming interface to the Systems Application Architecture systems. This interface consists of the languages and services used to develop productively applications that can be integrated with other applications and ported to run in multiple IBM Systems Application Architecture environments.

IBM is defining a Common Programming Interface that enables an application to be developed using IBM Systems Application Architecture products in one environment and then ported to another Systems Application Architecture environment with minimal changes to the application. This can result in increased programmer productivity and wider applicability of applications.

The initial elements of the Common Programming Interface are

- COBOL

  Based on ANS (American National Standard) Programming Language COBOL, X3.23–1985 Intermediate Level.

- FORTRAN

  Based on ANS Programming Language FORTRAN, 77 level.

- C

  Based on the draft proposed ANS Standard (X3J11).

- Application Generator

  Based on elements of the interfaces found in the existing Cross System product.

- Procedures Language

  Based on the existing REXX language.

- Database Interface

  Based on the ANS Database Language SQL, X3.135–1986, and IBM's SQL (Structured Query Language).

- Query Interface

  Based on an extension of the interfaces found in today's Query Management Facility (QMF) product.

- Presentation Interface

  Based on extensions to the interface found in key elements of today's Graphical Data Display Manager (GDDM) product, provides services to present textual and graphic information on displays, printers, and plotters.

- Dialog Interface

  Based on extensions to the interface found in today's EZ-VU product, provides for the definition, display, and management of textual information and menus, and for the control of screen flow within applications.

This Common Programming Interface provides a basis for customers and independent software vendors to use IBM Systems Application Architecture products to develop portable applications. Additional elements will be defined and the elements named above will be extended. The long-range goal is to define a comprehensive and productive set of IBM programming development languages and services.

Common Communications Support: Common Communications Support is used to interconnect Systems Application Architecture applications, Systems Application Architecture systems, communication networks, and devices. This will be achieved by the consistent implementation of designated communication architectures in each of the Systems Application

Architecture environments. The architectures announced here are the building blocks for distributed function to be detailed in future announcements of Common Programming Interfaces and IBM Systems Application Architecture applications.

The architectures selected have been chosen largely from Systems Network Architecture (SNA) and international standards. Each was also included in the Open Communications Architectures announcement of September 16, 1986 (Programming Announcement 286-410), thus reaffirming IBM's commitment to openness.

As IBM expands the Systems Application Architecture, additional communications architectures will be evaluated for inclusion in Common Communications Support.

Included in Common Communications Support at this time are:

Data Streams:

- 3270 Data Stream

  The 3270 Data Stream consists of user-provided data and commands, as well as control information that governs the way data are handled and formatted by IBM displays and printers. The Systems Application Architecture computing environments will all support the 3270 Data Stream. In addition, the System/3X family will continue to support the 5250 Data Stream. The 3270 Data Stream is documented in the IBM 3270 *Information Display System Data Stream Programmers's Reference* (GA23-0059).

- Document Content Architecture

  Document Content Architecture defines the rules for specifying the form and meaning of a text document. It provides for uniform interchange of textual information in the office environment and consists of format elements optimized for document revision. This is documented in *Document Content Architecture: Revisable-Form-Text Reference* (SC23-0758).

- Intelligent Printer Data Stream (IPDS)

  IPDS is the high-function data stream intended for use with all points addressable page printers. Planned availability for documentation of this data stream is third quarter of 1987.

Application Services:

- SNA Distribution Services (SNADS)

  SNADS provides an asynchronous distribution capability in an SNA network, thereby avoiding the need for active sessions between the end points. SNADS is documented in *Systems Network Architecture Format and Protocol Reference Manual: Distribution Services* (SC30-3098).

- Document Interchange Architecture (DIA)

  DIA provides a set of protocols that define several common office functions performed cooperatively by IBM products. This is documented in *Document Interchange Architecture: Technical Reference* (SC23-0781).

- SNA Network Management Architecture

  SNA Network Management Architecture describes IBM's approach to managing communication networks. The protocols of problem management offer a vehicle for monitoring network operations from a central location. This is documented in *Format and Protocol Reference Manual: Management Services* (SC30-3346).

Session Services:

- LU Type 6.2

  LU Type 6.2 is a program-to-program communication protocol. It defines a rich set of interprogram communication services including a base subset and optional supplementary services. Support of the base is included in IBM LU6.2 products that expose an LU6.2 application programming interface. This ensures compatibility of communication functions across systems. LU6.2 is documented in *Systems Network Architecture: Format and Protocol Reference Manual, Architecture Logic for LU Type 6.2* (SC30-3269).

Network:

- Low-Entry Networking Node

  A SNA *Low-Entry Networking Node* (Type 2.1 node) supports peer-to-peer communication. Type 2.1 nodes can be either programmable or fixed function systems. SNA Low-Entry Networking allows, through a common set of protocols, multiple and parallel SNA sessions to be established between Type 2.1 nodes that are directly attached to each other. Low-Entry Networking is documented in *Systems Network Architecture Format and Protocol Reference Manual: Architecture Logic for Type 2.1 Nodes* (SC30-3422).

- X.25

  X.25 defines a packet-mode interface for attaching data terminal equipment (DTE) such as host computers, communication controllers, and terminals to packet-switched data networks. An IBM-defined external specification, *The X.25 Interface for Attaching SNA Nodes to Packet-Switched Data Networks General Information Manual* (GA27-3345) and the 1984 version of this interface (GA27-3761), describe the elements of CCITT X.25 that are applicable to IBM SNA products that can attach to X.25 networks.

Data Link Controls:

- Synchronous Data Link Control (SDLC)

  SDLC is a discipline for managing synchronous, code-transparent, serial-by-bit information transfer between nodes that are joined by telecommunication links. This is documented in *IBM Synchronous Data Link Control Concepts* (GA27-3093).

- IBM Token-Ring Network

  The *IBM Token-Ring Network* consists of a wiring system (the IBM Cabling System), a set of communication adapters (stations), and an access protocol that controls the sharing of the physical medium by the stations attached to the LAN. The IBM Token-Ring Architecture is based on the IEEE 802.2 and 802.5 standards. This is documented in *Token-Ring Network Architecture Reference* (part number 6165877).

Common Applications: It is IBM's intent to develop common applications across the Systems Application Architecture environments. The initial focus is on office applications and, later, industry-specific applications. With the publications that define the IBM Systems Application Architecture and the availability of products, IBM is encouraging independent software vendors and customers to develop applications based on IBM Systems Application Architecture products.

As with the Common Programming Interface, elements are being defined for office applications. The elements being defined include:

- Document Creation
- Document Library
- Personal Services Mail
- Decision Support

Summary

IBM Systems Application Architecture is a set of software interfaces, conventions, and protocols—a framework for productively designing and developing applications with cross-system consistency. Systems Application Architecture defines the foundation to build portable, consistent application systems for the future with IBM hardware, control programs, and IBM Systems Application Architecture products.

Publications:

The following publications are the primary deliverables planned for the Systems Application Architecture in 1987:

- *Systems Application Architecture Overview* (GA26-4341)

  This publication introduces Systems Application Architecture concepts and provides the initial designation of the systems and products participating in Systems Application Architecture. Planned availability is second quarter of 1987.

- Common User Access Publication

  A reference manual is planned to be available in the third quarter of 1987. It will specify the common user access interfaces for intelligent workstations. Specifications for common user access interfaces for mainframe interactive terminals is planned to be added to this specification in the fourth quarter of

1987. The elements to be specified include screen layout, menu presentation and selection techniques, keyboard layout and use, and display options.

• Common Programming Interface Publications

Reference manuals are planned to describe each interface that participates in application enabling for Systems Application Architecture. These reference manuals will provide the grammar and syntax (supplemented by the programming guidance provided by the products that implement the interface) needed to develop applications for the Systems Application Architecture environments. The publications and their planned availability dates follow:

Title	**Available**
Common Programming Interface COBOL Reference	3Q87
Common Programming Interface FORTRAN Reference	3Q87
Common Programming Interface C Reference	3Q87
Common Programming Interface Procedures Language Reference	3Q87
Common Programming Interface Application Generator Reference	3Q87
Common Programming Interface Query Reference	3Q87
Common Programming Interface Database Reference	3Q87
Common Programming Interface Presentation Reference	3Q87
Common Programming Interface Dialog Reference	3Q87

- Writing Portable Programs

  This publication provides guidance on developing application programs that are consistent and portable among Systems Application Architecture systems. These applications will use the common Programming Interfaces and implement the Systems Application Architecture Common User Access specification. Planned availability is third quarter of 1987.

- Common Communications Support Publication

  The section Common Communications Support names the publications that define Systems Application Architecture communications protocols and standards.

Index

215

TK 7800. I14

BKS.
4fl

QA 76.8. I10 5 I245

QA 76.9. A73K 54

About the Author

Michael Killen is president of Killen & Associates, Inc., a consulting firm that specializes in forecasting the impact of IBM and AT&T's strategies on the corporate end user. He is the author of the highly regarded behind-the-scenes account of SAA, *IBM: The Making of the Common View*, has served as the co-host of a popular television program entitled "High Technology with Killen and Class," and speaks widely on developing information systems for the 1990s.